General editor: Graham Hand

Brodie's Notes on James Joyce's

A Portrait of the Artist as a Young Man

Graham Handley

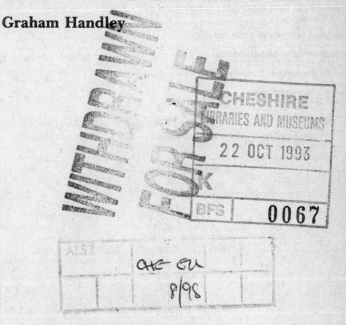

150th YEAR

M

MACMILLAN

First published 1977 by Pan Books Ltd

This revised edition published 1993 by
THE MACMILLAN PRESS LTD
Houndmills, Basingstoke, Hampshire RG21 2XS
and London
Companies and representatives
throughout the world

ISBN 0–333–58133–4

Typeset by Footnote Graphics, Warminster, Wiltshire
Printed in Great Britain by
Cox & Wyman Ltd, Reading

Contents

Preface

The intention throughout this study aid is to stimulate and guide, to encourage your involvement in the book, and to develop informed responses and a sure understanding of the main details.

Brodie's Notes provide a clear outline of the play or novel's plot, followed by act, scene, or chapter summaries and/or commentaries. These are designed to emphasize the most important literary and factual details. Poems, stories or non-fiction texts combine brief summary with critical commentary on individual aspects or common features of the genre being examined. Textual notes define what is difficult or obscure and emphasize literary qualities. Revision questions are set at appropriate points to test your ability to appreciate the prescribed book and to write accurately and relevantly about it.

In addition, each of these Notes includes a critical appreciation of the author's art. This covers such major elements as characterization, style, structure, setting and themes. Poems are examined technically – rhyme, rhythm, for instance. In fact, any important aspect of the prescribed work will be evaluated. The aim is to send you back to the text you are studying.

Each study aid concludes with a series of general questions which require a detailed knowledge of the book: some of these questions may invite comparison with other books, some will be suitable for coursework exercises, and some could be adapted to work you are doing on another book or books. Each study aid has been adapted to meet the needs of the current examination requirements. They provide a basic, individual and imaginative response to the work being studied, and it is hoped that they will stimulate you to acquire disciplined reading habits and critical fluency.

Graham Handley 1990

Page references in these Notes are to the Panther edition of *A Portrait of the Artist as a Young Man*, but references are also given to particular chapters, so that the Notes may be used with any edition of the book.

The author and his work

James Joyce was born in Dublin in 1882, one of a large family. His father sent him to a Jesuit boarding school, but was, as J. I. M. Stewart observes, 'sufficiently improvident to be virtually penniless a few years later'. This accounts for Joyce's transfer to Belvedere College, a Catholic day school in the city, although he was able to go on to the Royal University (University College, Dublin) in 1898. He graduated in 1902 with a degree in modern languages. Determined to turn his back on Ireland and establish himself on the continent, he studied medicine for a short time in Paris, but his mother's fatal illness in 1903 brought him back to Dublin. In June 1904 he met and fell in love with Nora Barnacle, a twenty-year-old girl who was working as a chambermaid in a hotel. In October 1904 they went to Italy, settling in Trieste in the spring of 1905, where Joyce began teaching English. Apart from a short spell during which Joyce worked as a bank clerk in Rome, they remained in Trieste until 1915 (they were not in fact married until 1931). They had two children, a boy and a girl.

Even before he abandoned Ireland, Joyce had started work on his autobiographical novel, 'Stephen Hero', which he was later to reshape and considerably reduce to the exact proportions of *A Portrait of the Artist as a Young Man*, referred to throughout this commentary as *A Portrait*. He was also to write a number of short stories, afterwards to be collected together under the title *Dubliners*, which were sent to the publisher, Grant Richards, as early as 1905. Because of the publisher's caution, however, and lengthy wranglings with printers, these were not published until 1914. Meanwhile, in 1907, Joyce had published a slim volume of verse, *Chamber Music*. *A Portrait* was serialized in an English magazine, *The Egoist*, in 1914–15, and in 1914 Joyce wrote most of his play, *Exiles*, which was revived by the Royal Shakespeare Company at the Aldwych Theatre in 1971, following a production at the Mermaid Theatre in 1970.

In 1915 the Joyces, now in financial difficulties, moved to Zurich. They received help from the Royal Literary Fund and the Civil List, as well as from two Americans, Harriet Shaw Weaver and Mrs Edith McCormick. Joyce returned to Trieste after the end of the First World War, but in 1920 he settled in Paris, largely at the instigation of Ezra Pound, his mentor and supporter over the years. *Ulysses* appeared in part in the *Little Review*, and was eventually published – in time for Joyce's fortieth birthday – in Paris in 1922, under the auspices of another American friend, Sylvia Beach. The publicity attendant upon its publication, and the subsequent court action in the United States to determine whether or not it was pornographic, brought Joyce an unwelcome notoriety. The woman who shared his life, but perhaps not his literary predilections, was to utter words which might be said to summarize the attitude of the uninformed general public at the time – 'I guess the man's a genius, but what a dirty mind he has, hasn't he?'. But an enlightened judge upheld the artistic integrity of the work, and *Ulysses* was published in America in 1934 and in England in 1936.

Joyce continued with 'Work in Progress', which was ultimately to be called *Finnegans Wake*, but during this period he was seriously worried about the condition of his daughter, Lucia, who was later to be admitted to a mental hospital. *Finnegans Wake*, a vast and bewildering work, alternately towering, comic and frustratingly idiosyncratic, was published in 1939, and was received without enthusiasm except by the select few who had charted its progress. Joyce eventually returned to Zurich, where he died in 1941 after an operation for an ulcer. His wife outlived him by ten years.

Joyce is a great writer of fiction and like some other major novelists, has become the centre of a research industry. Millions of words have been written about him and are to be variously valued according to their scholarship and critical astringency. Joyce invites such treatment, for his style, like T. S. Eliot's, is *allusive*, informed with a vast reading both ancient and modern, English and European. The reader of *A Portrait* is faced not only with new techniques but also with relating Joyce to the practice and concerns of his predecessors in the art of fiction. The presence of the author in the narrative in his own voice is central to Dickens, Thackeray and George Eliot, for example, but in *A Portrait* Stephen speaks of the artist as being 'impersonal'. One is aware here of the influence of the French novelist, Flaubert, with his concept of the detached reporter. As we read *A Portrait* we shall see that Joyce uses ironic and detached appraisal on the one hand while on the other he exposes his hero's consciousness with dramatic immediacy. *A Portrait* is the seemingly objective portrayal of an intensely subjective revelation.

From the above, the reader will have an idea of the complexity to be expected in Joyce, yet there is a tremendous enjoyment for the reader of *A Portrait* who is *not* bent on solving the multiple jigsaws of Joyce's style. That style is direct, objective, imbued with what he called 'meanness' in *Dubliners*, and the reader of this study aid is strongly advised to look at those stories as well as at *Chamber Music*, for both the stories of the one and the poems of the other were written while 'Stephen Hero', the precursor of *A Portrait*, was taking shape. The poems show how carefully Joyce had studied the Elizabethan writers. The poems are economical and lyrical, exhibiting that meticulous concern for words and their nuances which characterizes Joyce's manner in prose. What they lack is the fullness of feeling which was to animate *A Portrait*. *Dubliners* is equally important for the student. Joyce described it as 'a chapter of the moral history of my country ... the centre of paralysis', and the detached observer may dwell on the variants of that paralysis. The sordid and degrading aspects of life are written in a style consonant with their themes – spare, incisive, finely chiselled, drily ironic. But the last of these stories, 'The Dead', is longer, subtler, and appears to have a greater emotional involvement. It is a promise of the great writing to come, but here the tone is a compound of irony and compassion. Gabriel Conroy, filled with desire for his wife on the night of a party they have just attended, finds when they reach their hotel room, that she has been greatly moved by a song, which had been sung to her in the distant past by her consumptive, dead lover, Michael Furey. The climax of the story, with the dead present both in and to the living, and the dead Ireland buried in its length and breadth under a massive fall of snow, is superb, at once personal and symbolic, a blend of the poetic and realistic, psychologically true, but with associations beyond the immediate context.

All this is true of *A Portrait*. Read it straight through as narrative the first time, and see in which ways Joyce departs from his predecessors. Is Stephen's childhood presented in the same way as childhood in Dickens, for example? Has the author a moral standpoint which he is anxious to get across to the reader? Is there a plot in the sense we use the term? Are we concerned more with inward or outward events? Look at another novel, published just a couple of years before *A Portrait: Sons and Lovers*. In what ways does that novel differ from *A Portrait* in narrative method, characterization, style and emotional tone? The reader of *A Portrait* should read alertly, his or her imaginative eye seeing into the small and the large experience.

When he was eighteen years old Joyce wrote of Ibsen, the Norwegian dramatist whom he so admired, that one of his plays was 'in one way, so confined, and, in another way, so vast', and he also said that Ibsen 'presents his men and women passing through different soul-crises'. Both these judgments could be applied to *A Portrait*, that singular investigation of childhood, adolescence, the conscious and the subconscious, the sordid and the spiritual, the mundane and the ideal.

Setting and background

Personal

Patricia Hutchins has said that 'Joyce never tried to write outside the framework of his early environment and was obliged ... to convey its implications'. This statement applies particularly to *A Portrait*. Although the autobiographical element should not be stressed too strongly, since we are studying a book which has been deliberately cast in the form of a novel, certain basic identifications may help the reader to appreciate the authenticity of the background. A much more detailed examination is to be found in Patrica Hutchins's *James Joyce's World*, (Methuen), which is strongly recommended to the student who wishes to saturate himself in the atmosphere of Joyce's times.

John Joyce, the father of the writer, lived in Cork in his youth and was educated at St Coleman's College. Afterwards he studied medicine, attending Queen's College in the city. Joyce himself visited Cork as a small boy with his father, but the account he gives in *A Portrait* is probably updated from a later visit to the city in 1909. This provides the basis for the section devoted to the stay in Cork in Chapter 2, when Mr Dedalus (John Joyce) goes back for the sale of his property, another biographical detail used by the author. Similar examples of events taken from Joyce's personal background can be found at every turn in *A Portrait*.

The Joyces were living in Bray when James went to Clongowes Wood in 1888 and, since Parnell's death occurs in 1891, the Christmas dinner would appear to be at about this time, before their move to Blackrock in 1892. Here Stephen, his father and Uncle Charles go for long walks on Sundays, and there is every reason to believe that this was the practice of John Joyce and young James, and that the park where

Stephen does his 'running' under tutelage of Mike Flynn is at Tock Hill. By 1894, however, the move to Dublin had been made and it was here, according to Joyce's brother, Stanislaus, that the descent into eventual abject poverty was accelerated. In that year the family lived in Fitzgibbon Street; James was sent to Belvedere School, which was run by the Society of Jesus. This is paralleled by Stephen's changed circumstances and educational move in *A Portrait*. In 1895 the family was living in Drumcondra, and by 1901 (there is much skipping of time in *A Portrait*) they were at Fairview. It is in this year that Joyce (and hence Stephen) completes his first year at University College. The college was conducted by the Society of Jesus during Joyce's time too.

This, then, is the immediate background to the action of *A Portrait*. The much wider background, present in Stephen's mind in the infirmary at Clongowes and at the Christmas dinner, is concerned with the Church and Parnell

Political and religious

Charles Stewart Parnell was born in County Wicklow in June 1846. There was some anti-British feeling in his family, but despite this he was sent to boarding schools in England, and then to Cambridge. He was suspended in 1868 for a minor offence, and decided not to return to the University. A Protestant, he was elected to Parliament as a Home Rule League candidate in 1875. A man of impressive figure and a fine speaker, he consistently obstructed the English legislative process. By 1877 he was the most conspicuous figure in Irish politics, and was elected President of the Home Rule Confederation. In 1879 the Fenian Michael Davitt (mentioned in *A Portrait*) founded the Irish Land League and Parnell promptly identified himself with it. In 1880 the House of Lords rejected a measure for moderate land reform, and Parnell organized a massive land agitation which won the support of the clergy and of moderate opinion. Thirty-six Irish

Members of Parliament were suspended. Gladstone introduced his Land Act, Parnell tested it, making several inflammatory speeches, and in October 1881 he was arrested. Meanwhile, the suppression of the Land League in Ireland led to local terrorism, and ultimately the government came to realize that only Parnell could restore order. While in gaol his popularity was at its height, and he was known as the 'uncrowned king of Ireland'. Thanks to the offices of Captain William O'Shea, a moderate Home Rule Member whose wife had been Parnell's mistress since 1880, Parnell was released on 2nd May 1882. The attendant celebrations were short-lived, for on 6th May the Chief Secretary, Lord Frederick Cavendish and his Under-secretary, Henry Burke, newly appointed to Ireland, were murdered as they were crossing Phoenix Park, Dublin. Parnell immediately denounced the murders, and as a result fell out with the Fenians. He opposed the Prevention of Crimes Bill which was introduced in the House of Commons, and the Land League was revived in October. The situation was not improved by terrorist acts in England from 1883–5, but in 1886 Gladstone introduced his Home Rule Bill for Ireland. It was defeated, and Parnell allied himself with the Liberals who were now in opposition.

Then, in 1887, letters were published in *The Times* which apparently proved that Parnell was implicated in the Phoenix Park murders. A court case followed, and Parnell's innocence was proved by the confession of Richard Piggott, who fled the country and committed suicide in Madrid. Meanwhile, Captain O'Shea sued for divorce and Parnell did not bother to contest the case. He had apparently miscalculated the effects of the publicity. Gladstone disowned him and, though the Liberal Party nominally stood by him after the divorce, of the Irish members forty-five deserted him and twenty-six supported him. He fought on, but on 4th December 1890 he was formally repudiated by the Catholic Bishop and the archbishops. He continued to campaign, attracting large audiences wherever he went, but died in 1891 after a short illness.

It seems he brought about his own death by the excessive vigour of his campaigning and the prolonged travelling he undertook.

Parnell was effectively a martyr and, given the above outlines of his career, one can understand the conflict at table in *A Portrait* when Dante defends the Catholic viewpoint and Mr Casey sobs for his dead 'King'. Already subject to internal divisions, Ireland was further bedevilled by the controversy surrounding its lost leader.

Mythical

This is an essential element in Joyce's work, and one which is seen, at its most significant in *Ulysses*, as many commentators have demonstrated. *Dedalus* is a deliberatey chosen name, and Stephen ponders on it with increasing awareness as his sense of vocation becomes clearer to him. It will be useful to the student to look closely at the Daedalus myth, particularly the labyrinth and Icarus aspects of it.

Daedalus (which means 'cunning workman') was a skilled Athenian craftsman. He grew jealous of his nephew Talus, who was also his pupil, because the latter had invented the potter's wheel and the saw. Daedalus killed him, and Talus was changed into a partridge. Condemned for his crime, Daedalus fled to Crete where he built the labyrinth for Minos. However, Daedalus himself was confined to the maze with his son Icarus. He used his known ingenuity and built wings for himself and his son out of wax and feathers. They flew away, but Icarus flew too near the sun, the wax melted, he fell into the sea and drowned. Daedalus escaped to Sicily. Minos pursued him there, but met with a violent death. Connections with *A Portrait* will perhaps suggest themselves to the student; for example, Stephen is a craftsman with words and has to fashion his art, the labyrinth is perhaps the maze of Ireland with its politics and religion, though there can be no suggestion that the Church is the Minotaur. Is Stephen also Icarus – will he fly too near the sun and fall?

These then are the three backgrounds to the novel – the biographical, the political and religious, and the mythical. All three extend the text and indicate the imaginative and artistic dimensions within which Joyce worked.

Chapter summaries, critical commentary, textual notes and revision questions

Chapter 1 (pp. 7–54)

The first chapter opens with Stephen's earliest memories, beginning with his father telling him a story, his singing of a remembered song, his experience of wetting the bed and his preference for his mother over his father. Thereafter there is a movement through childhood – his reminiscences of his Uncle Charles, of Dante, of his neighbours the Vances, and their daughter Eileen.

The sequence is broken, and we are carried forward in time to Stephen's experiences in school and his reactions to them. He has bad sight, thinks of particular boys and their questions, and thinks, too, of his own early concern with words, and of his leave-taking of his mother and father. He contrasts school and the unpleasantness of it with the warmth of his home, but his lessons and the competitive nature of school also bulk largely in his consciousness. He is particularly aware of colours; aware, too, of misery, of the exchanges with other boys, of coldness and the 'slime' of the ditch, of his early geography lessons, of God and prayer and going to bed, of looking forward to going home in the holidays, of the legend associated with the school. He thinks specifically of the journey home but becomes feverishly ill, and has to be kept in the infirmary. Here he thinks of writing home, and later gets to know another boy called Athy; before that, however, he has experienced the prospect of dying, and this leads directly to his vision of the death of the great Irish political leader, Charles Stewart Parnell. See the section on *Political and religious background*.

We next find Stephen at home for Christmas. The party consists of his father (Simon), his mother, his Uncle Charles,

Dante (Mrs Riordan) and Mr Casey. Stephen, the eldest son, says Grace, listens to the conversation (speculating about certain words and their associations and meanings) and finds himself listening to a family row which Mrs Dedalus tries in vain to stifle. Dante attacks Parnell and defends the Church's attitude towards him while Mr Dedalus and Mr Casey stoutly affirm Parnell's loyalty and the Church's betrayal of him. Thus Ireland, with its divisions and its tribulations, is early impressed upon Stephen's mind and sensibility.

The chapter continues with another section of Stephen's life at school, with the 'fellows' talking about some boys who are supposed to have drunk altar wine, and Stephen is set thinking by association of his own visit to the little altar in the wood. This is followed by a dramatic return to the present: Stephen has broken his glasses, but his sense of hearing is good and he hears the fellows talking about what the boys really did – they were caught 'smugging' (masturbating) – but Stephen at the time doesn't understand what is meant by this. A number of associations with whiteness are set up in Stephen's mind – sweets, Eileen's hands, and the square (urinal) about which the other boys have been talking. After they have discussed the punishments which the boys will receive, they go into the classroom.

Father Arnall reprimands the class because of the appalling standard of the themebooks, the Prefect of Studies enters and first Fleming, then Stephen, the latter unjustly, are pandied (caned). We feel acutely the sensitivity of Stephen's reactions to this vivid, upsetting incident; the boys urge him to complain to the Rector, and this he does after much soul-searching, apprehension and, finally, determination and courage. He is kindly received, and the Rector promises to speak to Father Dolan about the wrongful punishment. Stephen is quite a hero among his schoolmates, and the chapter closes with the noise of ball on cricket bat from the fields.

The first section is typical of Joyce's methods in *A Portrait*. The consciousness is exposed in a series of recollections which have the force of immediacy, as if things were happening at that very moment. The main emphasis is on the various aspects of Stephen's sensitivity, encapsulated in his consciousness and his memory. Joyce's fascination with language, pronunciations and childhood reactions is evident. The short sentences reflect the disconnected nature of the experiences. The use of song and its effects, both in the structure of the novel and as revelatory of Stephen's experiences, is given in the notes below. Note the class awareness which characterizes many of Stephen's experiences at school, and also the emphasis on the senses – reactions to cold, warmth, comfort, and the incidence of fear which occurs so regularly. Joyce has captured perfectly and with remarkable associations the actuality of childhood experiences. The slang of the period and the place is convincing, adding to the feeling of immediacy. What Joyce is exploring is the nature of childhood, the obsessive imaginings which occupy the passing moment ('Was it right to kiss his mother or wrong to kiss his mother?') in all their terrifying power. Stephen's intensely inquiring mind mirrors that of his creator, while in the family disagreement one sees the mirror of Ireland, at this stage not comprehended by Stephen but central to his awareness as he grows from child to young man. The portrait, in other words, is being gradually filled out, and we see in fact the compulsive effect of religion in the nature of his prayers and his fears, with a prefiguring too of the conditioning and obsessive period of his later youth. Notice how the change of mood from fear to joy is registered by the natural outbursts of this joy and then a sequence which is expressive of serenity through the rhythms of the prose. But because of the time switches in the narrative there is a brilliant exposure of Stephen's delirium in sickness, and in the infirmary scene the anguish of his insecurity. Joyce's psychological consistency in the presentation of Stephen is remarkable, even to the romantic sentimentality and the death-wish of the sensitive boy. The incidence of questioning and self-questioning returns – the fascination with facts and words which constitute the active imagination of the child. Stephen's vision, or rather his capacity for imaginative association, even embraces the death of Parnell and, like a dream we have just had, links with the present as well, another instance of Joyce's complete identification with his subject. The Christmas dinner exchange of course symbolizes the divisions of Ireland: it also reveals much of Mr Dedalus's attitudess towards life (and religion and politics) and of the attitude of Stephen towards him. Stephen's sense of pride, and his apprehensions at what is *his* first Christmas dinner, are well conveyed. The argument is fast and furious, underlining the fact that the differences are irreconcilable. What is superbly conveyed is the isolation, fear and bewilderment of the child trapped in the grown-up situation. The mixture of emotions renders the scene compelling and poignant, with the coarseness of Mr Dedalus evident, and Mr Casey's support fuelling the scorn and derision, the child a silent spectator of the adult war. But what adds immeasurably to the power of the scene is its universality, our knowledge that Christmas, a celebration, is so often typified by family quarrels. Joyce is once again displaying his knowledge of human nature: this is not just an insular Catholic family, but *any* family in interaction (I say *any* not *all*). Note how convincing the dialogue is. Casey is deliberately provocative, and Joyce is building up the atmosphere of disagreement which sours the seasonal celebration. The act of spitting is itself a degradation, while the recital of names is a kind of self-convincing name-dropping on which to rear irrational argument. In some ways the movement of the argument prefigures Stephen's own development, for he is later to pass through the allure of religion to its rejection. With Mr Casey's sob and his father's tears Stephen partly apprehends this fully-charged moment of emotion, here a notation of his own development. The sequence which follows the Christmas dinner is rich in symbolism, of flouting the church by drinking and stealing, of masturbation, the sin of self-abuse or the indulgence of sensuality, but the irony is that Stephen,

who cannot see, because of his broken glasses, cannot see
either, yet, in terms of understanding. In a sense Joyce's
account is one of innocence exposed to a world of half-
experience, half because not properly understood. Notice that
the blurring of sight is compensated for by the sense of hearing, and of touch. Stephen's musing on what has happened
leads once more to imaginative associations which prefigure
his later temptation: altar wine sets up pagan images ('the
grapes were dark purple that grew in Greece outside houses
like white temples'). Stephen's ever-active mind, always questioning, considers whether Father Arnall sins by being 'in a
wax', and it is this kind of question which leads ultimately to
his rejection of religion: there is a quiet humour too in his
tracing an ascending order of confession. The caning is one of
the most graphic and moving sequences in the book, an indictment of those who act unjustly in the name of discipline and in
the name of religion: additionally it is an indictment of cor-
poral punishment, which hurts the body but more importantly
scars the mind. Stephen's dissociation from his hands and his
moving personification of them again underlines the terrible
immediacy of the scene. It is a major event in Stephen's
development, with the sense of humiliation perhaps upper-
most. We note the reaction of Father Arnall in his quiet tones,
but are aware that it is too late. I have said above that this is a
formative moment for Stephen, and one of the ironies attending it is the fact that he becomes one of 'them', his group of
boys, and ceases to be the outsider he so obviously is because
of his innocence, a certain effeminate quality, and his lack of
ability at games. Notice though that his conception of protest
draws on the literary or religious analogies that are the natural
accompaniment to his thoughts and, here, his emotions.
Stephen also faces the temptation of not doing anything, and
it is a measure of his courage that he goes through with it.
Joyce is here, as so often, building up a tense atmosphere
through the apprehensions of Stephen: but even at this crisis
we note his awareness of language – his pondering on the

name of Dolan, for example. Stephen's movement through the corridor with the other boys watching him shows Joyce using the effects of silence as dramatic contrast to the tumult within. The interview with the rector reveals the other side of the religious coin: Stephen has the courage and the stamina, despite his tears, to see it through to the end, and both he and the rector observe a code of loyalty, of honour. Stephen's running, and the boys' shouts, are a mark of acceptance, of achievement even. Most interesting is Stephen's reaction after the triumph: his feeling that he would like to do something 'kind' for Father Dolan is true to life, expressive of our own need to be accepted on *all* levels, or as many as we can. The last paragraph, which looks back to an earlier sequence, conveys a kind of serenity; Joyce cleverly uses this as contrast with the previous mood.

pp. 7–31
Once upon a time The traditional way of beginning a story *for* children; ironically, this is one *about* a child.
through a glass A monocle.
lemon platt i.e. 'plaited' sticks of sweet tasting of lemon.
O, the wild rose ... O, the green wothe Song forms a great part of the background in this novel, and here the red and green motif is first mentioned. One thinks immediately of blood and the Emerald Isle, of conflict recurring. Stephen sings his song lispingly, sleepily, and therefore slurs and disarranges the syllables.
sailor's hornpipe Dance involving a single person, associated with sailors celebrating.
Dante His 'baby name' for his aunt and a reference to the poet who, like his aunt, was a fervent Roman Catholic.
press Large, shelved cupboard, usually in the recess of a wall.
cachou A pill used to sweeten the breath.
Pull out his eyes ... Apologize Notice first of all the bird image, though here with a menacing association (eagles) and the fact that this poem symbolizes revolt – for Stephen's rejection of what is expected gives rise to it. It contrasts immediately with the innocent song which is *his* song and it also anticipates his later rebellion.
The wide playgrounds This effectively marks the beginning of a new section: Stephen's move to Clongowes.

flew like a heavy bird Images of birds run through *A Portrait*. They become progressively more attractive as Stephen begins to find himself.

his eyes were weak and watery Important because Stephen, like Joyce, has poor sight, but the quality of his inward vision – his imagination – is, if anything, enhanced.

stink i.e. unpleasant.

greaves in his number Each boy had a locker – Roddy Kickham kept his shin-guards in his.

dog-in-the-blanket Rolled currant dumpling or jam pudding.

belted ... belt Already Stephen's awareness shows.

your match i.e. someone your own size, your equal.

a toe in the rump i.e. a kick in the bottom.

fiveshilling Notice that Joyce frequently dispenses with the hyphen and runs two words into one.

peach Inform against, turn informer.

soutane Priest's cassock.

seventy-seven to seventy-six i.e. the number of days before the holidays. Stephen does change this later.

Hamilton Rowan (1751–1834) The Irish patriot who hid at Clongowes and succeeded in throwing the pursuing English soldiers off the scent.

ha-ha A sunk fence, or ditch, around parkland or gardens.

slugs Irregular shaped bullets.

Leicester Abbey – *Wolsey* (1471–1530). The latter was Henry VIII's Cardinal. He was arrested for High Treason, was taken ill on the way to London, and died at Leicester Abbey with the famous words on his lips: 'Had I but served God as I have served the King. He would not have forsaken me in my grey hairs'.

Doctor Cornwell's Spelling Book Standard manual for the learning of spelling in the nineteenth century.

Mozambique Channel In Portuguese East Africa, as it then was, visited by St Francis Xavier.

one last i.e. kick.

suck Once again, Stephen's early word awareness. Here it means 'sucked up to'.

the prefect's false sleeves The reference is to the Prefect of Studies and to the extra sleeves of his long gown. His judgment, too, is false, as we can see when he pandies Stephen.

like a little song Stephen uses the image – perhaps it looks back to the 'little song' which Stephen regards as his. It underlines his loneliness here.

York – ... Lancaster The two houses in the Wars of the Roses (1453–86). The badge of the former was white, of the latter red.

Henry VII united the claims of both in his person when he succeeded to the throne after the battle of Bosworth.

a wax A temper.

blue sailor top This form of shirt-like garment was fashionable at the time.

elements This would be the first, or 'elementary', class from which Stephen would graduate into 'third of grammar' and thence up the school.

clumsy scullion, girt with Notice the style change here – the language is dated, old-fashioned, perhaps like Clongowes itself.

hogwash i.e. fit only for pigs.

sick in your breadbasket Slang for 'you have a stomach-ache'.

like a train One of Stephen's favourite comparisons; he is often thinking of journeys – all of which lead to his final decision.

Dalkey Suburb of Dublin. Joyce taught there for a short time in 1903.

Tullabeg Jesuit school closed earlier, the pupils moving on to Clongowes.

a big rat jump plop into the scum This image, and others connected with it, are repeated several times to indicate Stephen's sensitivity.

but one time it would come Notice how Joyce gets inside a young child's mind.

green ... maroon Another mention (and they are frequent) of one of the recurring motifs.

a cod A hoax.

Stephen Dedalus ... heaven my expectation Even this simple verse carries its particular irony, for Stephen is to leave Ireland and, before that, to reject the way to heaven.

Dieu Again the whole sequence round this word shows Stephen's childlike concern with words.

It was like a train going in and out of tunnels One of Stephen's favourite images as a child. Ironically it looks forward to his train journeys from Blackrock to Dublin and from Dublin to Cork, both of which are sad.

so that he might not go to hell when he died This reflects childish fear. The fact that the idea has been drummed into him may account for Stephen's later rejection of the Jesuits.

the white cloak of a marshal This is a reference to a legend that one of the previous owners appeared as a ghost to the servants. He was supposedly killed at the Battle of Prague (1757).

Visit, we beseech thee Notice this interpolation of a fragment of prayer to underline the child's fear.

cars Wheeled vehicles, horse-drawn.

a long long chocolate train with cream facings The image is

Stephen's, and perhaps reflects his desire for sweets after the Clongowes food.

red holly ... green ivy Again the reference, with associations of the shedding of blood perhaps. The red-coated soldiers of England, the green flag, the Emerald Isle – these run through the text on various levels.

Sorry because he was afraid The rest of this sequence is 'stream of consciousness', with Stephen's thoughts jumbled together.

foxing i.e. pretending.

Father Minister Priest in charge, responsible to the Rector.

collywobbles Joyce is adept at capturing the slang cliché, and many occur in the infirmary sequence. Strictly this word means 'rumbling in the intestines'.

Brother Michael Not ordained, a lay brother.

Hayfoot! Strawfoot! Equivalent of *Left right! Left right!* Derived from the American Civil War.

Butter you up! Again the cliché slang, here meaning 'Make a fuss of'.

walking papers i.e. discharge, have to return to school.

when Little had died A real contemporary of Joyce's at Clongowes.

cope A long cloak worn by ecclesiastics in processions.

Dingdong! The castle bell! Look carefully at this song, with its 'Farewell, my mother!' which anticipates Stephen's ultimate departure, not to death but to life.

spiffing Slang for 'fine, first-rate'.

a thigh A play of words, but Stephen, always interested in words, will not say the answer because he is sensitive – and perhaps wants Athy to have the pleasure of telling him what it is.

that riddle another way Stephen is too naive to see what Athy is getting at – the leg could be a female's just as well as a fellow's.

the liberator Daniel O'Connell (1775–1847) was known by this name. He took his seat in the House of Commons in 1829, and was renowned for his physical strength.

themes Close study of nouns and verbs, particularly involved with the adding of inflexions.

lovely foreign names in it Stephen always has a wish to travel, and this is one of the early manifestations of it. But notice once more that he is interested in the words!

He saw the sea This is again from the consciousness, but it is in the form of a dream or vision.

Dante in a maroon velvet dress By association, in the dream, Dante is for Davitt and not Parnell, which is why she walks 'proudly and silently' past the people who are kneeling in respect to the dead Parnell. This dream anticipates the next section and its conflict – the Christmas dinner.

in a jiffy Slang again, meaning 'soon'.

toasted boss The footstool, which was very warm.

those three cramped fingers making a birthday present for Queen Victoria The original on which Casey was modelled had spent some time in prison and claimed to have damaged his fingers.

ozone Here Mr Dedalus is referring to the refreshing air.

bedad Irish version of 'By God'.

manufacturirng that champagne The implication may be that the hotel-keeper is a swindler, or even that he has been involved in something of which Dante would not approve.

my hearty i.e. my good fellow.

pearled ... with glistening drops Somewhat commonplace poetic image.

the real Ally Daly That's the pick of the lot.

Eton jacket A boy's short coat reaching only to the waist.

lopsided Uneven, i.e. he is more dishonest than honest.

any sauce Mrs Dedalus is speaking practically, but Mr Dedalus is certain to give Mrs Riordan 'sauce' in the conversational exchanges to come.

pity the poor blind i.e. forgive me for not seeing.

Right as the mail i.e. just right.

I'll pay your dues The implication is that the speaker will attend church when the priest ceases to take politics as his theme there.

Were we to desert him The reference is, of course, to Parnell. (See the section on *Political and religious background*.) Other references are to Parnell's adultery.

Woe be to the man In fact Mrs Riordan is referring to Luke 17, 1 and 2.

pope's nose The rump of the bird, equivalent to the 'parson's nose'.

I'm not well in my health lately Mr Dedalus is ironically referring to his lack of spiritual health.

Billy with the lip ... the tub of guts up in Armagh Insulting remarks about two leading Catholic churchmen who had helped to bring down Parnell – the Archbishop of Dublin and the Bishop of Armagh.

Lord Leitrim's coachman Mr Dedalus is being sarcastic, for Lord Leitrim had been murdered by what he regarded as *loyal* Irish, and the coachman who tried to defend his much-hated Englishman would, in Mr Dedalus's eyes, be a traitor.

pp. 32–54

like rats in a sewer Ironically, Mr Dedalus uses a figure of speech much in Stephen's mind!

crooning like a country singer This, and the two lines he sings, are calculated to provoke Dante by their irreverent tone.

spoiled nun i.e. one who intended to be a nun, but gave up because of the rigours of the life.

chainies Irish dialect plural of 'china'.

the litany of the Blessed Virgin ... Tower of Ivory ... House of Gold Both are present in the Litany as marks of purity and rarity.

long white hands Notice how the association of 'white' has set Stephen on a sensual train of thought.

tig A game in which one person tries to touch the other players.

Arklow Coastal town south of Dublin

the chief died i.e. Parnell.

harridan A vixen (of a woman).

The Paris Funds! Mr Fox! Kitty O'Shea! This is running the gamut of Parnell's supposed misdemeanours. He was accused of taking money for himself, money held in Paris for the National League, and he sometimes assumed the name of Mr Fox when meeting Kitty O'Shea.

a quid of Tullamore A lump of tobacco, presumably originating from the town of that name.

chinstrap Passing under the jaw, thus holding (the cap) in place.

till the end of the chapter i.e. until things come to an end.

as a whiteboy The whiteboys were a secret Irish organization and, in the 1760s, they perpetrated certain outrages. They were named after the white smocks they wore on their nightly raids.

mahogany Table.

Bishop Lanigan ... Marquess Cornwallis The Lord Lieutenant of Ireland who resigned in 1801 because he had promised Catholic Emancipation but the King (George III) had withheld his Royal assent. Lanigan believed that the Catholics were to be emancipated, hence his address of loyalty. The Catholic Emancipation Act was passed in 1829; certainly the Church opposed the Fenian movement because of its emphasis on freeing Ireland by force of arms. Throughout this, and in order to provoke Dante, Mr Dedalus is taking the extreme view.

Terence Bellew MacManus See the note below on Paul Cullen. MacManus, who had taken part in the 1848 rebellion, died in America, but his body was brought back to Ireland and there was a public funeral.

Paul Cullen (1803–78) Irish Cardinal, Primate of Ireland: against Irish Nationalism, but failed to prevent the public funeral of MacManus.

no God for Ireland! These words, uttered in the passion of the moment, have a long term effect in the action of *A Portrait*, for Stephen is ultimately to reject God *and* Ireland.

as though he were tearing aside a cobweb Joyce is adept at the casually effective image.

We crushed him to death Again, the reference is to Parnell.

his father's eyes were full of tears Mr Dedalus is often emotional, sentimental. Later Stephen is to be ashamed of this.

higher line i.e. Upper school.

fecked Stolen.

scut Fled.

sacristy Place for keeping vessels and vestments of the church.

crimped Compressed into plaits or folds.

boatbearer i.e. the boy who carried the vessel which held the incense.

machine i.e. bicycle.

prof A *prof*essional cricket coach for the school. One wonders if the reference could be to the legendary S. F. Barnes.

pick, pack, pock, puck: little drops of water Stephen, his sight impaired, takes great pleasure in the sounds he can hear, and the image invests them with a poetic significance. He is to repeat the exact phrasing later.

the square The area which enclosed the toilets.

Smugging i.e. masturbating. Stephen reveals that he has no idea what Athy is talking about.

always at his nails, paring them Ironic that the effeminate Boyle should practise what Stephen sees as one of the attributes of the artist.

She had put her hand into his pocket Eileen is a little precocious, perhaps sexually aware; Stephen manifestly is not.

By thinking of things you could understand them This reflection shows Stephen's capacity to work out his ultimate salvation.

Balbus was building a wall A simple Latin construction.

backhand i.e. with the strokes of the letters sloping backwards.

Julius Caesar wrote The Calico Belly Schoolboy parody of the Latin for Caesar's *Concerning the Gallic Wars*.

and the way he said it Stephen ponders, but is too naive to grasp the implication.

six and eight i.e. strokes of the cane.

ferulae Strokes with the teacher's stick.

It's best of his play not to It would be wise of him (not to flog hard).

It can't be helped Typically proverbial schoolboy verse – it contrasts with some of the more serious verses in the novel, with the songs as well – and, ironically, it looks forward to Stephen's own pandying.

But that was not why Stephen's sensitivity tells him that Mr Gleeson is basically gentle.

fine invisible threads Further stress on Stephen's weak eyesight.

monstrance Open or transparent vessel in which the Host is exposed. It is of gold or silver.

Napoleon There are several references to Napoleon in the text. The great French emperor and general was born in Corsica in 1769, and died after six years' imprisonment on St Helena in 1821.

mare Sea.

ablative The case in Latin nouns that expresses the source, agent, cause or instrument of action.

provincial ... general Ranks of the Jesuit order in ascending importance.

the prefect of studies i.e. the Jesuit in charge of academic work.

pandybat A rod of reinforced cane.

Tomorrow and tomorrow and tomorrow Ironic that the Prefect of Studies should echo Macbeth's famous soliloquy after the death of Lady Macbeth. Not to put too fine a point on it, Macbeth is a murderer; the prefect here is murdering peace of mind and ruling, like Macbeth, by fear.

Lazy little schemer The irony, one feels, is unconscious, but since the Prefect of Studies repeats Stephen's name twice he may be thinking of *the* Daedalus, who was certainly a schemer. (See section on *Mythical background*.)

no-coloured A fine way of indicating the terrible impersonality of the man who is determined to punish.

a leaf in the fire ... a loose leaf in the air Note how both images underline the fragility of Stephen's hand and of his mind, which is suffering.

as if they were not his own Again Joyce's fine ability to capture the nature of momentary reaction.

unfair and cruel Note the repetition of the phrase – we tend to repeat things when we are suffering over and over again, almost as a reflex to our emotional or physical pain.

The senate and the Roman people declared A common enough reference to the literature they would be studying, but updated to fit Stephen's case.

Richmal Magnall's Questions A question and answer history textbook which went into many editions in the nineteenth century.

Peter Parley's Tales The pseudonym of S. Goodrich, who wrote books of stories from classical history for children.

Dolan: it was like the name of a woman who washed clothes

It is; but the expression of it here shows Stephen's snobbery and sense of his own difference.

Ignatius Loyola The founder of the Jesuits (1492–1556).

Ad Majorem Dei Gloriam 'For the greater glory of God.'

Francis Xavier (1506–52) Jesuit missionary, associated with Ignatius Loyola, he christianized much of the East.

Lorenzo Ricci Born in Florence, a Jesuit general who, when the order was suppressed, retired to St Angelo, where he died in 1775.

berretta Round, black, close-fitting skull-cap.

Stanislaus Kostka (1550–68), of Polish origin.

Aloysius Gonzago (1568–91), Jesuit saint, mentioned again near the end of the novel.

Blessed John Berchmans (1599–1621), canonized in 1888, the patron saint of young altar boys.

Father Peter Kenny Hardly as elevated as those mentioned above – he was the founder of Clongowes.

pick, pack The repetition which reflects Stephen's being at peace with the world.

Chapter 2 (pp. 55–94)

Stephen is at Blackrock with his Uncle Charles. He is 'trained' by his father's old friend, Mike Flynn, and on Sundays goes for long walks with his father and Uncle Charles. He reads, becoming particularly fascinated by Dumas's *The Count of Monte Cristo*, and plays, creating adventures with a boy called Aubrey Mills. He begins to dream of Mercedes, the heroine of *The Count of Monte Cristo*, and becomes aware of the changes in his father's circumstances. He is not sent back to school at Clongowes, and the family leaves Blackrock and moves to Dublin. Stephen is initially bewildered by the 'vastness and strangeness' of the city; he becomes aware both of stirrings and inadequacies within himself, he remembers with strange vividness certain experiences, he tastes the degradation of poverty. He begins to write, and then learns that he is to go to Belvedere, a Jesuit college.

Next, Stephen is about to act in a play and intently watches the preparations for it. He talks to his friend Heron and then, being lightly struck with a cane, recalls another incident earlier in his life when he had been baited and assaulted by three of his schoolmates. After the performance of the play he leaves quickly, partly to avoid his father but also because he wishes to be alone.

The next sequence finds Stephen and his father on a trip to Cork – a trip full of memories and drinking for his father, and full of sensitive jarrings for Stephen. He is sickened by himself and by the oppressive advice his father presumes to give him. He is deeply concerned about the sin within himself, realizes that his father's property is being sold, and feels keenly his isolation from his father and the latter's drinking cronies. He feels that he has had nothing of their life or youth, and we are told that 'Nothing stirred within his soul but a cold and cruel and loveless lust'.

Stephen gains an exhibition and wins an essay prize, spending lavishly on his parents while he can. But he soon tastes disgust again and, driven by lust and the strength of his desires, finally goes to a prostitute and surrenders himself to her, body and mind.

Fundamentally, this second chapter traces the stirrings, the frustrations, the heightened intensity of emotion, shame and sexuality in an adolescent boy.

Note the comment made at the end of the summary above, and consider the selective use of particular scenes to heighten our knowledge of Stephen through the nature of his differing experiences and his growing into a fuller awareness. The training sessions with Mike Flynn are inlaid with humour, but there is also a marked sadness and seediness about them too, with the feeling that for Uncle Charles and Flynn life is virtually over. Again notice Joyce's concentration on particularities, the 'long swollen fingers' of Flynn, for example. Sad irony attends the prayers of Uncle Charles, but we are made aware of the ever-present interest of Stephen in words, here seen as he listens with 'an avid ear' to what is being said. Even more important is the half-awareness Stephen has that he will achieve something, and the influence of his reading upon the romantic turmoil of his imagination. The small whitewashed house is a focus for his dreams: more practical – and boyish – is the adventure seeking with Aubrey Mills, almost as if the physical and the imaginative life must be balanced or harmonized in some way. The description of the cowyard reflects Stephen's incapacity to face everyday sordid reality (and, later it will be more personally immediate than this). The return to Mercedes' image is accompanied by restlessness and idealized visions of love which he cannot articulate. The vision means for him the loss of 'Weakness and timidity and inexperience'. The emotional identification with Stephen's moods is remarkable. The change of circumstances is conveyed through mood reactions. Again we are aware of the complete identification of the author with his creature, and the experience of Dublin fuels the restlessness which his imagination had experienced earlier. The mood is generally one of frustration and discontent, a feeling of inadequacy. A series of epiphanies emphasizes the various forms that these moods of frustration take. The incident on the tram with Eileen is brilliantly evocative of sexual response and an attendant indecision. The scene and its finality is anticipatory of other failures. The beginnings of his poetry and his look into his mother's mirror reflect (the right word) his absorption with his physical and mental self and the image he has of that self. The conversation when Stephen learns that he is to go to Belvedere is revelatory of Mr Dedalus's boasting nature, the loud and swaggering outside which conceals his own failures. One wonders if his pride in the story about Father Dolan is more his own sense of being an anecdotal man rather than genuine appreciation of his son, whose sensitivity is certainly beyond him. The scene of the play is another fine piece of atmospheric writing. The old lady/young girl contrast forms another epiphany with telling effect – all is not what it seems, a reminder of deceptions in life (and self-deceptions in life) and the fact that the play itself is a representation not a reality. The parody greeting of Stephen is ominous, for these boys are enacting a little play off-stage, so to speak. The incident over the interpretation of the essay anticipates Stephen's later rebellion, while the argument about poetry shows the boys trying to subdue Stephen, the outsider, who does not conform to their practices or appreciate them. Yet his reaction – that he does not hate his tormentors for what they have just done – shows just how remarkable he is. The switch back in time to the theatre sequence noted in the summary above again shows Joyce's deliberate undercutting of ordinary time and his replacing it with sequences which evolve through association. Most important is the phrase 'Another nature seemed to have been lent him' as he is being made up to go on stage – and here Joyce has conveyed the sudden transitions, as so often, of Stephen's moods. His reaction after the performance, that of getting away quickly, is entirely natural. He is anxious for reality, however sordid, and we register the contrast with his earlier rejection of the filthy cowyard. The song and its theme are typical of Mr Dedalus, since for him this is an indulgence of the past. Stephen's sensitivity to atmosphere and the vividness of his imagination are shown in the anatomy theatre. The child in the womb – the carving of *Foetus* on the desk sets Stephen's imagination tracing his own sensual images of love – if you like, his imagination ironically begets dreams as physical love begets children. The father–son interaction is being spelled out, with Mr Dedalus's outward show, Stephen's inward brooding, a clear underlining of the generation gap. The further irony is of course that Mr Dedalus feels that they are more like brothers. His constant recurrence to the past is the measure of his failure to live in the present. Stephen's own return to the past is riddled with insecurity and uncertainty as they walk along together – his only certainty is in the use of language, particularly, to anchor himself both in the past and the present. Joyce captures perfectly the conversations and their innuendo, both of which make Stephen uncomfortable. The boasting and the drinking of his father with these 'cronies' sets Stephen even further apart: as always, he withdraws into himself, feeling the onset of guilt and shame which characterize his intense subjectivity. The spending of his prize money shows the inherent generosity of Stephen, and at the same time his impetuosity and family awareness. Here Joyce's prose is crowded with what he does, as if each word is one of the coins spent to purchase some gratification for his family – and himself. Particularly effective here is the use of water imagery to convey his reactions to what he has done. The sequence of Stephen's wanderings, both in fact and imagination, is superbly done: Joyce has here captured the tensions of the mood of self-indictment, for Stephen often feels in extremes, and the extremity of self-judgment is almost a commonplace with him. As I have said in the notes below, the sequence with the woman shows his vulnerability, his youth, his need for love obvious between the lines as a counterbalance to his lust. Again, the prose in which this sequence is written perfectly conveys the state of Stephen's mind and the onrush, ultimately to swooning, of his sensuality.

sounding-box i.e. in which to test his singing.
O, twine me a bower, Blue Eyes and Golden Hair Irish songs; the latter provided the melody for Moore's *The Last Rose of Summer*.
The Groves of Blarney Air by R. A. Millikin, written about 1700.
Blackrock The Joyces lived at Blackrock for about eighteen months in 1892–3.
Stillorgan Five miles from the centre of Dublin where Leopardstown Racecourse is.
Munster A reference to the harbour in Tipperary.
the great part which he felt awaited him It is all the more ironic that it is only shortly after he feels these stirrings in himself that the family poverty descends upon him.
The Count of Monte Cristo By Alexandre Dumas (the elder); one of the most celebrated of his stories, published in 1844. 'That wonderful island cave' is where the treasure is hidden in the novel. Mercedes ultimately repents her betrayal of the Count.
Marseille Major French city and port on the Mediterranean.
Madam, I never eat muscatel grapes This statement, a quotation from the novel, symbolizes the Count's rejection in his maturity of Mercedes – he refuses to eat what she offers.

in that moment of supreme tenderness he would be transfigured Stephen is very romantic at this stage (probably influenced by Dumas) and feels that with his ideal beloved he will lose all shyness and awkwardness.

revery Day-dreaming.

There's a crack of the whip i.e. I've got some life left.

We're not dead yet See the note above. Mr Dedalus often repeats himself in clichés.

on the quays and on the river The restlessness which leads ultimately to his decision to quit Ireland, and the new poverty he is experiencing, is evident here.

He chronicled with patience He takes note of what he sees, and certain things remain with him for him to savour – the three scenes which follow immediately upon this (epiphanies, in fact) – are good examples of this. The first concerns the beautiful Mabel Hunter, the second the appearance of the deranged or simple girl, and the third the tram sequence with E–C–.

mud Dialect, short for 'mother'.

the ways of adventure that lay open in the coals i.e. he is looking into the fire and letting his imagination work.

A skull appeared suspended Note the effect of someone disembodied, unhinged. It is startling.

cowled head Significant description, for a cowl is properly a monk's hooded garment, and this perhaps suggests E–C–'s later religious interests.

like a cork upon a tide An echo of Stephen's visit to the Dublin docks.

in some dim past, whether in life or revery We suspect that it is the romantic past with Mercedes in *The Count of Monte Cristo*.

he had yielded to them a thousand times i.e. in his imagination.

he remembered the day when he and Eileen He remembers his innocence and shyness then, and this makes him withdraw from contact with E–C–, despite his wish to kiss her.

the jesuit motto A.M.D.G. As we have seen, this stands for 'For the greater glory of God', and he writes it, as he would do in school, at the head of his poetic 'exercise'.

Lord Byron (1788–1824). Stephen's early favourite and, like him, an exile from his country. Byron left England in 1816 and never returned.

Bray The Joyces moved there in about 1888. It is on the coast just south of Dublin.

second moiety notices i.e. those asking for the payment of rates.

L.D.S. The abbreviation for the Latin phrase *Laus Deo Semper* – written at the completion of the formal exercise in school. Habits die hard with Stephen. It means 'Praise be to God always'.

that his father would make him dip his bread i.e. in the interests of their new economy nothing must be wasted.

coated ... with a scum of disgust Note that the 'scum' was much feared by Stephen at Clongowes after he had been shouldered into it by Wells.

Belvedere In reality, this Jesuit school was only ten minutes walk from the Joyces' home in Dublin.

Christian brothers ... Paddy Stink and Micky Mud This order then taught the children of the poor, and Mr Dedalus is being contemptuous of the kind of children Stephen would have met if he had gone to them.

put your shoulder to the wheel i.e. begin to work hard.

mumbled Chewed.

the Whitsuntide play Stephen's performance is based on fact, for Joyce himself had taken off his headmaster in a play.

farcical pedagogue Ridiculous teacher, probably very pedantic.

Neapolitan peasants i.e. dressed like peasants from Naples, presumably a group of dancers.

a festive ark, anchored ... frail cables ... moorings A fine sequence of connected images which reflect Stephen's wish, later translated into fact, to escape by travel. The images are continued at the end of this paragraph.

dwarf artillery Stephen always has an acute ear for sound, and this is an apt description of the sound of artillery when heard from a distance.

Here comes the noble Dedalus ... Welcome to our trusty friend There is a Shakespearean echo to this.

salaamed 'Made a mock bow' perhaps renders the word accurately here.

ripping Heron, like Athy, indulges in a good deal of slang. The word means 'marvellous'.

beads i.e. the Rosary.

a sly dog i.e. secretive, keeps things quiet.

the stream of gloomy tenderness ... dark courses and eddies Here the sequence is to be equated with Stephen's emotion at the thought of seeing E–C– again.

one sure five i.e. 'that's certain'.

Confiteor Prayer confessing sins.

a sudden memory This is the beginning of a retrospect, rather like the flashback technique of the cinema. Joyce frequently uses it.

before they passed out of it into his crude writings The implication is that Stephen, in his new poverty and crude company, does not yet write well.

read his fate in the incidents ... in the spaces of the patchwork of the pathway Notice how finely Joyce causes the reader to identify with Stephen and his mood of uncertainty – the day changes for each of us according to our own code of superstitions.

his turned and jagged collar From now on Joyce includes in the text short but effective references to Stephen's poverty and its effect on the boy. Here is Stephen's collar compared with Mr Tate's 'heavily starched' one.

Drumcondra Road The Joyces lived near here at the same time as Stephen attended Belvedere.

Captain Marryat (1792–1848) Perhaps best remembered for *Mr Midshipman Easy* and *The Children of the New Forest*.

Fudge Slang for 'rubbish'.

Newman (1801–90). Started the Tractarian movement in 1833, advocating High Church principles and practice, but became a Catholic in 1843. Head of Birmingham Oratory 1849. Cardinal 1879. Fine prose writer (see *Apologia Pro Vita Sua* and *The Idea of a University*).

Lord Tennyson (1809–92) Born in Lincolnshire, generally unsuccessful until the publication of *In Memoriam* in 1849. He became Poet Laureate in 1850 on the death of Wordsworth. Stephen is reacting as a romantic young man would – for the Romantic poet, Byron, against the Victorian poet, Tennyson.

Alec Kafoozelum A nonsense name for the sake of the rhyme.

a trans Presumably an abbreviation for 'translation'.

While he was still repeating We have now moved back to the present, just before Stephen takes part in the play.

like an invisible wave Again the image is used to convey his emotion, here his passion.

bally Expressing disgust or satisfaction, a polite form of 'bloody'.

While his mind had been pursuing A very important paragraph, for it traces Stephen's isolation; his rejection of being a gentleman, a good Catholic, an athlete, a nationalist; and the need for him to retrieve his father's fallen fortunes.

The Lily of Killarney The opera by Julius Benedict written in 1863.

the simple body i.e. the audience as a whole.

mummery His actor's clothes and accessories.

like crushed herbs in his heart As Stephen matures, and as his emotions and his imagination become more intensely evocative, so the language of his experiences becomes more poetic.

Lotts The name of the lane in which he finds himself.

like fiery grains flung backwards by a runner Stephen is thinking both of the cinder track at Clongowes and of his previous 'training' under Mike Flynn.

the purpose of his actual visit i.e. the auction of his property.

Maryborough ... Mallow The first a small, the latter a large town north of Cork.

the telegraph-poles held the galloping notes of the music between punctual bars Vivid image which captures the regularity of the rhythm.

jingle A carriage drawn by horses.

Tis youth and folly Obviously a popular Irish song, but 'bonny' is substituted by 'bony'; Mr Dedalus in a good mood is sometimes witty.

festooned Imaginative usage, here meaning 'adorned'.

come-all-yous Typical opening of Irish popular songs.

grace notes Embellishments of extra notes not strictly needed for the harmony or melody.

drisheens A pudding with meat.

the Mardyke The main road.

Foetus Fully developed embryo in the womb.

His monstrous reveries Stephen has guilt feelings about his sexual desires and dreams.

Groceries A shop.

the squalor of his life and against the riot of his mind i.e. his poverty and his wish to indulge himself sexually. Stephen's guilt makes him put things in extremes, and just after this he refers to his 'mad and filthy orgies'.

a good actor, another could sing a good comic song Stephen is later to credit his father with all these qualities, but not without a satirical intention.

maneens Young fellows.

I am Stephen Dedalus ... Names A pathetic attempt to establish a balanced perspective by repeating facts to allay the 'riot of his mind'.

slim jim A kind of sweetmeat made in long strips.

like a film in the sun Fine economic image to convey the way the past is erased by the present.

a lob The meaning of this is uncertain. However, beggars ask for money, so this could be a coin, or just a 'hand-out'.

Peter Pickackafax A jocular coinage, a talking down to Stephen.

jackeen Youngster.

curvetings Springing about, perhaps twisting and turning.

the Lee ... the Liffey The rivers of Cork and Dublin respectively.

Dilectus There is no such writer, so the old man is displaying his own lack of real knowledge.

Tempora mutantur Two versions of 'The times change and we are changed with them'.

He's not that way built Ironic, in view of Stephen's 'orgies'. 'He isn't inclined that way.'

Sunday's Well Suburb of Cork.

Art though pale for weariness This quotation is from Shelley's fragment 'To the Moon', written in 1820.

the house of commons of the old Irish parliament A reference to the Bank of Ireland acquiring the building.

Hely Hutchinson and Flood and Henry Grattan and Charles Kendal Bushe Irish elected members of Parliament who spoke their minds.

they are only as I roved out one fine May morning in the merry month of sweet July Mr Dedalus is speaking flippantly, using a reference to a song to convey the temporary nature of things.

Ingomar or ***The Lady of Lyons*** The first a melodrama which had been translated from German, enjoyed some popularity in the nineteenth century. The second was written by Lord Lytton and produced in 1838.

desuetude A state of disuse.

breakwater … tide of life … dam up … barriers … crumbled mole The water imagery superbly conveys the movement of lust with him. A 'mole' is a structure of stone used as a breakwater.

mystical kingship of fosterage This is almost wish-fulfilment, the need to distance himself from them which is to crystallize later.

Only the morning pained him The whole of the preceding paragraph is a fine analysis of an adolescent's guilt over his awakening sexuality – the lustful wishes, masturbation, 'wet' dreams. Bearing in mind the time at which *A Portrait* was written and published, it is a remarkable description.

Mercedes Stephen sees himself returning, like the Count of Monte Cristo, but he sees himself, too, as Claude Melnotte, hero of *The Lady of Lyons*. Part of his reaction against his poverty is the escapist wish for noble birth. Notice how the word 'holy' is used in the imaginary account of his meeting with his dream beloved, and how it contrasts with the actual reactions of his mind.

the echo of an obscene scrawl Urinals often contain words or drawings which are a sordid, lustful comment on sex, reducing it to its lowest level. The whole of Stephen's inward tummult here shows his guilt feelings (sin is often mentioned), his lust (flood, streams) which is seen too in terms of animal passion (prowling beast). It is all the prelude to his finding a prostitute.

lightsome Light, elegant in appearance.

He wanted to be held firmly in her arms We must not forget that in some ways Stephen is still a child; there is something maternal about this embrace.

Revision questions on Chapters 1 and 2

1 What strikes you as different about Joyce's style in these chapters? Refer closely to them and quote in your answer.

2 What impression have you formed of Stephen in these chapters?

3 Write an account of the Christmas dinner, bringing out clearly the reactions of each character.

4 What is for you the most moving incident in these chapters and why.

5 Write an essay on the nature of Stephen's relationship with his father.

6 Analyse any two or three epiphanies in this section, indicating what they contribute to the narrative.

Chapter 3 (pp. 95–133)

Stephen is in the schoolroom, lusting for food and for further sexual adventure; he looks at the page in front of him, but can only see his soul expanding in sin. He further ponders on sin and the nature of religion, and finds himself present at the retreat listening to a sermon on St Francis Xavier. After this Stephen indulges in extensive self-examination and self-blame, torturing himself for his sinfulness and his distance from God. Consequently the sermon which follows sears his soul, as the terrible prospects of Hell are explored in detail by the preacher. The impact on Stephen is both spiritual and physical, so that he leaves the chapel beaten, uncertain, acutely aware of his own unworthiness. The next sermon explores in equally terrifying detail the pain of loss, the pain of conscience, the pain of extension and intensity, of variety and eternity. At the end of it Stephen prays with all his heart, 'his tongue cleaving to his palate'. Later when he prays a fearful vision of devils comes upon him. Afterwards he walks through the streets of the city, the city of his sins of the flesh and the spirit, and goes to the confessional. The result is that all is transformed – he feels that 'God would enter his purified body' and 'The past was past'.

The focus is on Stephen's indulgence of the senses, food and sex almost equated in his mind as he yields himself up to creating scenes about which he knows through his own previous participation in them. We note the realism, both internal in his mind and external in the tarts' conversations. His recall of Shelley's poem is couched in poetic terms by Joyce, the space image contrasting with Stephen's containment, his being caught in the trap of selfhood and temptation. It is natural that his own transition should be from fallen women (and he regards himself as fallen) to the Virgin Mary. What is very effective here, as in so many parts of the novel, is the mixture of Stephen's inward temptations and his emergent spirituality with the everyday things going on around him which he finds disgusting. It is one of his main characteristics that he should constantly question and requestion himself. The sermon is so exactly captured that it almost becomes a parody – the references show Joyce's saturation in the Bible and in the teaching of the Jesuits. The reiteration of 'my dear little brothers in Christ' offers Stephen the innocence he has lost and for which he now craves. The rhetoric is resonant with authorities, the appeal is really a calculated one. The mass of physical images conveys the intensity of the spiritual/ emotional experience. Death imagery of a strongly visual quality is also present. Stephen's mind is shown in turmoil, and the religious insistence is seen as oppressive and irresistible. Colours – green, scarlet – are also used effectively, but the omnipresence of the sermon traps Stephen, with its rhetoric and repetitions evoking his sense of guilt. The death imagery here is also oppressive. Stephen's reactions include the feeling that he has died, though he soon realizes that he is back in the everyday world. But so intense is the language, so repetitious, turning and twisting, that we feel the personal force and above all the personal anguish which Stephen suffers. *A Portrait* is convincing throughout, but there is a frightening pressure about this sequence which conveys 'the threefold sting of conscience' in such a way as to make escape from spiritual/ moral responsibility impossible. Notice that the rhetoric is balanced by rhetorical questioning, the ebb and flow of the mind and the spirit as the full pressure of revelation and persuasion is unleashed. There is little wonder that Stephen becomes feverish, for he is passing through a delirium of experiences and fears, and we are reminded of his childhood fever in the infirmary when the anguish of being away from home and feeling threatened undermined him. The experience with the 'Goatish creatures' is a waking vision evoked by his ever-present guilt and fear, and containing his physical re- pugnance to filth (symbolic of his sins of the flesh) which we have seen before. The confession is movingly done, the priest's 'weary and old' voice conveying the inevitability of sin and its widespread currency – he has heard it all before. His need to believe strikes a note of genuine pathos – Stephen feels he has a new life, but the reader feels that he may be deluding himself.

eyed and starred like a peacock's Symbolic, perhaps of woman. But it is linked, as we see, to 'his own soul going forth to experience'.
surd Either means irrational (in Maths), or a sound uttered with the breath and not the voice.
sodality A confraternity of a religious character.
the little office A collection of biblical readings which were recited daily in honour of the Virgin Mary.
The glories of Mary A sermon by Cardinal Newman.

Quasi cedrus ... suavitatem odoris This is from the Little Office but there are errors in it. It is, as one would expect, in praise of the Virgin Mary.

bright and musical A quotation from *The Glories of Mary*.

My excellent friend Bombados Line from a current song.

That's game ball i.e. we shall be free to play.

The sentence of saint James The paraphrase refers to the General Epistle of James 2, 10: 'For whosoever shall keep the whole law, and yet offend in one point, he is guilty of all'.

The retreat Temporary retirement for religious exercises. In *A Portrait* it only occupies two days.

fold and fade with fear like a withering flower Notice how the alliterative use of 'f' conveys the tremulous, short-of-breath feeling that Stephen is experiencing.

Sancian Island off the Chinese mainland.

A great fisher of souls! From now on, biblical references are thick and fast in this chapter. The student will be able to identify many of them by the use of a *Corcordance to the Bible*, but the important thing to note is the way Joyce captures the *manner* of the preacher.

the simoom The hot, dry, suffocating wind that crosses the desert.

Ecclesiastes Contains no verse 40 in Chapter 7. The reference is to *Ecclesiasticus* in the Apocrypha.

became again a child's soul And the irony is that in doing so it becomes vulnerable, the prey to past (religious) associations.

What doth it profit a man ... St Mark 8, 36.

to be devoured by scuttling plumpbellied rats This is vividly present in Stephen's mind, but again it can be traced back to his childhood when he was shouldered into the square ditch.

The sun, the great luminary ... This whole sequence has a nightmare intensity in Stephen's mind.

Jehoshaphat Mentioned in Joel 3, the valley between Jerusalem and the Mount of Olives. From ancient times it has been a Jewish burial ground.

Addison The reference is to Joseph Addison (1672–1719), editor of the *Spectator* with Steele. In addition he wrote some beautiful hymns.

O grave where is thy victory? The quotation is from Alexander Pope's (1688–1744) poem 'The Dying Christian to his soul'.

Emma Elsewhere referred to as E–C–.

not like earthly beauty ... Another quotation from *The Glories of Mary*.

Hell has enlarged ... Here the hell-fire sermon begins in earnest. Joyce adapted much of the material in these paragraphs from a seventeenth-century Italian religious work. This he edited and, obviously, condensed.

Saint Anselm ... similitudes St Anselm (1033–1109), Archbishop of Canterbury, a fine-principled man. Similitudes are likenesses, outward appearances, comparisons.

The horror of this strait Much emphasis is placed in the sermon on a number of 'considerations'. This, the first, describes the prison of Hell.

Saint Bonaventure (1221–74) A mystic, ironically, greatly admired by Luther.

The torment of fire This is the second of the definitions – the nature of the fire of hell.

the company of the damned themselves The third quality of Hell.

Saint Catherine of Siena (1347–80) Patron Saint of the Dominican Order, celebrated for her ecstasies and visions, and for the marks of suffering which she bore on her body.

the temple of the Holy Ghost i.e. the body of man.

He came down ... his legs shaking This represents the break in the sermon, and Stephen's initial, fearful reaction to it.

the overcoats and waterproofs hung like gibbeted malefactors... Notice how, because of the power of the sermon, Stephen invests the commonplace with tremendous significance – here the garments are like hanging men, symbols of his own sin.

like a corolla A whorl of leaves.

blue funk (Made us) very frightened.

like a cold shining rapier The image is particularly effective since the suffering of the flesh is what Stephen is to wish for in the light of his sins.

He sat again... The continuation of the sermon.

the pain of loss The fourth of the sufferings of Hell.

Saint Thomas The reference is to Thomas Aquinas (1227–74). Joyce himself made a great study of his writings.

the pain of conscience The next of the sufferings.

Pope Innocent the Third (1160–1216) Generally regarded as the greatest of that name, he vastly extended the territorial power of the Church.

saint Augustine (354–430) The greatest of the Latin fathers of the Church.

the pain of extension The sixth of the sufferings of Hell.

the pain of intensity This co-exists with 'extension'. Taken together they mean continuing forever, with no diminishing of power. The result is hopelessness.

a great hall ... the ticking of a great clock ... ever, never;

ever, never ... The words, the repetitions, would have a particular force for Stephen, who is very aware of sound. Consider the *pack, puck, pock,* from the cricket field which is reiterated in his consciousness.

Will we trample again up on that torn and mangled corpse? Notice the number of rhetorical questions, indeed the nature of the repetitive rhetoric that runs through the passage. The words may be equated with the ritual – they are the verbal equivalent to it.

– *Oh my God!* – Notice that the prayer is repeated by the boys hence the repetition of the printed word on the page.

viscid Sticky, semi-fluid.

We knew perfectly well ... of course perfectly well The words appear to come from the 'eyes' and 'faces' who have waited for him in the darkness; perhaps they come from Stephen's consciousness, ending, as they began, the circle of his sin. We soon learn that the words 'had seemed to rise murmurously from the dark.'

A field of stiff weeds and thistles This is a kind of waking dream, with the stress on what is physically repugnant, something that has always worried Stephen from his earliest days in Clongowes.

grey as indiarubber Almost a casual simile from his daily experience in the schoolroom.

rictus Gape of a person's or animal's mouth.

lecherous goatish fiends Obviously he sees this kind of Hell because he feels his sins have been sexual.

the city was spinning about herself a soft cocoon of yellowish haze Again, even at this moment of crisis and agony, a superb poetic effect.

He once had meant to come on earth ... guide us home The paragraph is from *The Glories of Mary*, but with some adjustments.

sacristan Sexton of parish church.

capuchin A member of the Franciscan order.

like a sinful city ... Notice how the image is continued by the fever of the imagination.

like perfume streaming upwards from a heart of white rose Again, a subtle look back – remember that Stephen, when young and pure, wore the white rose of York at Clongowes.

And life lay all before him A half echo of the end of Milton's *Paradise Lost*, for the two sinners – 'The world was all before them'.

ciborium Silver cup, holding the consecrated wafers, in the Communion service.

Corpus Domini nostri ... In vitam eternam 'The body of our Lord ... to life everlasting.'

Chapter 4 (pp. 134–57)

Stephen is in the throes of his religious commitment, praying, reading, undertaking the 'lowliest devotion' and bringing each of his senses under the heel of his new discipline. He goes to see the Director, who implants in him the idea that the priesthood may be his true vocation. Now he is positively tempted, seeing himself as 'The Reverend Stephen Dedalus, S.J.'. He returns home to ponder, sitting with his brothers and sisters amid the poverty to which his family has been reduced. He then walks to the city, communing with himself, passing as he does so a squad of Christian brothers. Then from his memory, he finds a phrase: 'A day of dappled sea-borne clouds' and, looking out to sea, he undergoes a mystical experience, a new and heightened sense of awareness, which shapes his future.

He is brought back to reality by seeing some of his companions playing in the sea. When his name is called, the name of the 'fabulous artificer', he recognizes his destiny and is moved to reject 'the inhuman voice that had called him to the pale service of the altar'. He wades in the sea and experiences, in his new exalted state, a moment of unvoiced communion with a girl who is standing in the water. After this moment of ecstasy he sleeps on a sandhill, waking in the evening to the fullness of his joy.

It is in this section that Stephen begins to find himself, to discover the identity which his uncertainties have hitherto failed to define. In the first part of this chapter religious devotions are undertaken with complete commitment: such is Stephen's awareness of his self-sin that he ritualizes his day so that it is one long coherent devotion. This underlines his rational approach (see notes below) and his determination to put down his sensuality: he avoids the eyes of women, for example, but goes to extremes to deny himself the experiences of the other senses. We cannot help but feel that the attitude is one of negation, that in an attempt to elevate the religious he is destroying the natural. Again we feel he is undermined by the ordinary everyday occurrences (like the anger he feels at hearing his mother sneeze). The water imagery crucial to his coming discovery is employed before the physical actuality ('seeing the silver line of the flood far away...') but is here used to symbolize temptation. We feel that this is resisted but that it will return, and the Director's conversation with him in fact sets his mind again in movement towards the temptations of women. Even a phrase like 'the soul or body of a woman moving with tender life' indicates the nature of Stephen's feeling as well as his ever-present feeling for words. In fact the Joycean irony encompasses the idea that the real temptation is towards the priesthood, and the other temptations (seen as sin) are towards life. Yet Stephen himself, as he ponders the idea of entering the priesthood, is conscious of his own sin of pride, the lure of power. Nonetheless he contemplates a future in which he will hear confessions and be 'as sinless as the innocent'. In a superb epiphany of young men enjoying life together, Joyce evokes the contrast which is instrumental in moving Stephen towards rejection of 'The Reverend Stephen Dedalus, S.J.'. Stephen's return to the poverty of his family marks another stage in his development. Particularly effective is the distortion of the replies he gets to his question, and the singing which has a sadness of its own. Notice that Stephen adopts his own ritual in walking, and that the idea of finding himself through the university means that he is still searching for the right path. The whole of the last sequence in this chapter stresses the contrast between the crude realities of earthly living and the visionary experience of Stephen which is conveyed through the epiphanies. The epiphany of the girl causes Stephen to utter 'profane joy'. He has been freed by this experience from his religious chains, and the whole sequence suggests that the world of the imagination, drawing on the richness and beauty of life, will be given full expression.

In a few words, the artist will be free to paint his portraits.
This time water, the natural reality as distinct from the imagery,
serves to indicate both factual and imaginative journeying.

sovereign pontiff i.e. the Pope.

ejaculations Brief prayers.

supererogation A reserve fund of merit that can be drawn on in
favour of sinners.

like fingers the keyboard of a great cash register... This
image, which rings up pardons, is not without a certain cynicism
on the part of Joyce.

Paraclete The Comforter. (The Holy Ghost.)

save as a theorem of divine power... Notice the language,
for Stephen is always rational as well as spiritual.

the mortification of touch In this phase Stephen mortifies his
senses, but touch – from Eileen's hands onwards through sexual
experience – seems to him the most sinful of his senses.

stiffly at his sides like a runner Childhood is never far away for
Stephen. Remember his runs around the park at Blackrock
under the tutelage of Mike Flynn.

saint Alphonus Liguori (1696–1787) Barrister who became a
priest and eventually founded the Redemptorists, a group of
missionaries working in the Naples area.

sere foxpapered leaves i.e. dry, brown-stained pages.

the canticles Little songs, hymns.

Amana A mountain.

Inter ubera mea commorabitur 'He shall stay betwixt my
breasts' (Song of Solomon, 1, 13).

a flood slowly advancing... Image associated with passion,
here the movement of temptation.

looping the cord of the other blind The gesture seems symbolic
– almost as if the reflex action is 'snaring' Stephen.

dubitative Inclined to doubt or hesitation.

Les jupes Those wearing skirts.

muff Awkward or stupid.

Lord Macaulay (1800–59) The great essayist and historian who
had a remarkable memory.

Victor Hugo (1802–85) Celebrated French poet, novelist and
dramatist.

Louis Veuillot (1813–83) French journalist of strong Catholic
views.

genuflecting Bending the knee in worship.

thurible Censer, a vessel in which incense is burned.

chasuble Sleeveless vestment of celebrant at Mass or Eucharist.

tunicle Short vestment at Eucharist.

humeral veil Oblong silk scarf worn around priest's shoulders during part of the Mass.

paten Shallow dish used for bread at Eucharist.

dalmatic Wide-sleeved, loose, long vestment.

Ite, missa est Depart, the mass is ended.

Simon Magnus See Acts 8, verses 9 onwards, for an account of Simon's sorceries and his later attempt to gain, by bribery, the power of the laying on of hands.

Melchisedec This means 'King of righteousness'. (See Psalm 110, 4 – 'Thou art a priest for ever after the order of Melchisedec'.)

novena Special prayers or services on nine successive days.

a sudden wave dissolves the sand-built turrets of children Interesting image which looks forward to the sequence where Stephen sees the girl, but again temptation is present in it. An imposed way of life is a sandcastle to be broken.

Lantern Jaws ... Foxy Campbell Nicknames.

the faded blue shrine of the Blessed Virgin which stood fowl-wise... Patricia Hutchins recalls seeing the statue among the Tolka cottages when she went there, but it was later removed.

Tea was nearly over This whole paragraph is redolent of the sordid reality which Stephen faces. Having determined to reject the proffered hand of religion, he is determined to reject this too.

turnover Semi-circular pie or tart.

Goneboro... The double syllable which follows each word is typical of childish affectation – and it's also expressive of the monotony of their poor existence.

Oft in the Stilly Night Irish melody by Thomas Moore (1770–1852).

Newman ... Virgil The quotation is from Newman (see earlier note). Virgil (70–19 BC) is a Latin poet, author of the *Aeneid*, the *Georgics* and the *Eclogues*.

without regret of a first noiseless sundering of their lives The 'without regret' is very significant. Stephen has willed himself to follow what he thinks is the right path for himself.

like long slow waves... The familiar image, but used with rather a different emphasis.

Their feet passed in pattering tumult... Compare this sequence with the earlier one on p. 126, where the 'goatish creatures' are described. This is deliberate contrast to underline Stephen's sense of freedom through the imagery.

Whose feet are as the feet of harts... Fine extension of the above by direct quotation from Newman's *Idea of a University*.

tape-like collars i.e. very narrow ones.

A day of dappled seaborne clouds This is from a book by Hugh Miller. Miller (1802–56) was a journalist and geologist, born in Cromarty, and self-educated. As the phrase suggests, he had considerable literary ability.

Words ... lucid supple periodic prose This paragraph should be studied in detail as Stephen ponders on the associations of words, what they mean to him, how best he loves to hear them and see them.

infrahuman i.e. below the human.

spine of rocks ... river's mouth Marvellously economic image, part of Joyce's own 'lucid supple' poetic prose in this section.

arras Hanging screen of tapestry.

the seventh city of christendom ... thingmote Dublin, and its Danish Assembly in pre-Conquest times.

voyaging across the deserts of the sky ... Europe... Stephen's mind, like the clouds, is moving into new areas of contemplation.

A voice from beyond the world... The voice(s) Stephen actually hears are coarse and down to earth, so that his vision is tinged with irony.

a stuff in the kisser 'A punch in the mouth.'

Bous Stephanoumenos! Bous Stephaneforos! The ox with a garland! The ox, carrier of a garland! The punning connections with Stephen are obvious, since St Stephen (literally 'a garland') was the first Christian martyr. Stephen's awakening from his dream is a kind of martyrdom, and the comparisons of these boys with the 'goatish' people of his hell-fire vision are implicit (again see p. 126).

Norfolk coat A loose jacket with a waistband.

the ancient kingdom of the Danes... See note above on 'thingmote'.

the fabulous artificer See section on *Mythical background*, but study this whole paragraph carefully. Stephen, always aware of names and especially his own, is searching out his own future through the legend and its implications for himself.

he was soaring sunward... Like Icarus. The irony is far-reaching. Will Stephen himself be burned?

cripes Again the coarse voices cut across his vision and his elation. This means 'Christ'.

a lust of wandering This lust, both of the imagination and of physical travel, is not to be stilled.

Howth A place of cliffs, bays and woodland, with a famous castle.

her house of squalor and subterfuge to queen it in faded cerements The language reflects his own poverty and the way he 'buried' himself in the grave clothes of religious observance.

He was alone His isolation is stressed, but note the repetitions of this paragraph, the repetitions of ecstasy.

a girl stood before him ... This superb picture, imbued with the bird imagery which characterizes the flight of Stephen's imagination and the hope for his future, is at once poetic and mystical.

faint as the bells of sleep Another echo stretching back into childhood ('Dingdong! The castle bell! Farewell my mother!'). The second line is particularly relevant here, since Stephen's decision involves leaving his mother, spiritually and, later, in the flesh.

A world, a glimmer or a flower? A superb poetic conveying of ecstasy, a mood of exaltation at the richness of experience and the beauty of life. Here the repetitions are those of the moments before sleep.

the rim of a silver hoop embedded in grey sand This whole section is a poetic flow of consciousness, of mood expressed through images.

Revision questions on Chapters 3 and 4

1 Describe Stephen's religious phase in some detail.

2 Give an account of the sermon and the atmosphere captured here by Joyce through his stylistic effects.

3 Indicate the part played by water and water image in Stephen's discovery of himself.

4 Which do you consider the most important epiphany in this section and why?

Chapter 5 (pp. 158–228)

Chapter 5 finds Stephen at home in his stifling daily surroundings, elder brother of the younger children who must make way for him. He takes his morning walk across the city, late for his lecture, passing places and statues as he goes. He thinks back over his friendship with Davin who told him the story of his encounter with the woman on his walk back from Buttevant. Back in the present Stephen meets a flower-girl, walks on through St Stephen's Green and goes to see the Dean of Studies, a priest. Stephen realizes the futility of his discussion with the Dean and then attends a class, conscious of the coarse humour of his colleagues, until the bell. Stephen declines to sign a testimonial in the name of the Tsar calling for universal peace. There follows much talk with his fellow students, one or two of whom are intent upon baiting Stephen. The latter becomes friendly with Lynch, an impoverished student, and they discuss life, art and philosophy, not without humorous and satirical overtones.

They learn the results of the examinations from another student and Stephen discourses on the definition of beauty and of what it consists: wholeness, harmony and radiance. There is considerable discussion of the functions of words as they are used in different circumstances, a subject which is always of interest to Stephen. Gradually, he comes to his definition of the artist, the climax of his thought:

The artist, like the God of creation, remains within or behind or beyond or above his handiwork, invisible, refined out of existence, indifferent, paring his fingernails. (pp. 194–5)

He sees E–C– with the other students, but goes home and sleeps, waking to ideas and poetry, feeling, thinking words, composing, inspired. He writes his *villanelle* in sections, thinking of E–C– as he does so, becoming angry because of her interest in Father Moran. Then, returning to ecstatic contemplation and desire, he writes out the nineteen lines in full. Later he stands on the steps of the library, watching the birds in flight, moved by the augury they present. He thinks back to the opening of the Irish National Theatre, turns into the library and finds Cranly. There is a brief grotesque encounter with a dwarf, and Stephen's imagination follows associations set up in his mind by this meeting. After more talk with his fellows, he sees E–C– again, allows himself the indulgence of a number of images, and rejoins his companions. There is more conversation about religion, Stephen revealing to Cranly that he has quarrelled with his mother because of his disbelief and his refusal to attend to his observances. Cranly tries to undermine the quality of Stephen's rejection, but cannot do so.

Stephen tells Cranly that he will probably go away, that he will 'try to express myself in some mode of life or art as free as I can and as wholly as I can, using for my defence the only arms I allow myself to use – silence, exile, and cunning.' (p.222)

He has, in effect, confessed to Cranly. The last chapter moves irrevocably towards artistic definition and verbal decision. Its last part is given over to Stephen's diary entries, which contain occasional references to E–C–. Some of them are disjointed, grotesque and nightmarish. He records his meeting with E–C–, but the arms become 'white roads' in his mind, and he decides to go away into the 'reality of experience'. This coda witnesses the arrival of decision, the self-knowledge for Stephen that he must escape into this free air of the future. He has worked out a philosophy of creating and perhaps a philosophy of life, and now intends to embrace them both to the full. This means turning his back on home and on Ireland.

This final chapter marks the end of Stephen's quest, and thus the beginning of his future. He is still living with the sordid reality of poverty, and this sequence is a contrast with the uplifting experience with which the last chapter ends. Note how effectively conversation is used to convey the immediacy of monotonous, pointless existence, with Mrs Dedalus and Mr Dedalus pulled down by it. The sound of the mad nun adds a grotesque touch, but Stephen is now on the short walk (walks are important as a notation of what he feels) which precedes the long walk into the future – the journey from Ireland and into voluntary exile. There are some superb poetic phrases ('His mind was a dusk of doubt and mistrust').

His pondering on Cranly shows him again aware of the influence of religion on his behaviour, for his confiding in the 'priest' Cranly is compared to confession. This section is packed with reference, the evidence of Stephen's enquiring mind, his learning at the university, and it serves as an effective contrast to the priest's rhetoric earlier. Davin's story is couched in the language of temptation which Stephen knows so well. Note the symbolic description of Stephen's Green, while Stephen's interaction with his fellow students reveals Joyce's ear for natural, reflex humour, some of it ingenious, some of it coarse. Joyce is also mocking the pretentious nature of pseudo-learned discussion. But the running innuendo is that Stephen is gradually working his way towards discovery, towards fulfilment. Notice how the description of scene emphasizes the divisions between Stephen's wishes and life as it is ('the sluggish water and a smell of wet branches over their heads seemed to war against the course of Stephen's thought'). The writing of the *villanelle* is an important index to Stephen's development, his use of the past in his appraisal of the present, and his movement towards a fuller self-knowledge. The diary sequence with which the chapter ends shows the full nature of Stephen's mind, his thoughts of E–C– and his wonderful range of reference and detailed attention to language, its resonances and innuendoes. There are some brilliant word pictures, but most interesting of all is Stephen's self-knowledge about what he wants to do – 'The past is consumed in the present and the present is living only because it brings forth the future'. It effectively summarizes the practice of the artist, the continuum providing the material to which he will give shape and finality.

pp. 158–80
Buskins Boots reaching to the calf or the knee.
louse marks Note the way the *sordid* is contrasted with the *ecstatic* of the previous section.
The dear Mrs Dedalus always observing her religion, cannot bring herself to say 'the dear Lord'.

I'm going for blue Blue is a substance used by laundresses; the girl is obviously going out to get some to wash the clothes.

Gerhart Hauptmann (1862–1946) German dramatist in whom Joyce was greatly interested. Stephen is thinking of the romantic facets of Hauptmann's work.

sloblands Marshes.

cloistral silver-veined prose of Newman The number of references to Newman – and their tone – shows what a deep impression he made on Joyce.

Guido Cavalcanti (1250–1300) Italian poet, celebrated for the style of his romantic love poetry.

Ibsen (1828–1906) A Norwegian dramatist who had a great influence on the young Joyce, who wrote an essay on him. Ibsen was, as Joyce became, an exile.

Ben Jonson (1573–1637) Famous contemporary of Shakespeare, he was a poet and dramatist. The line is from the epilogue to one of his masques, *The Vision of Delight*.

Aristotle (385–322 BC) Chief writings were *The Politics* and *The Poetics*. He greatly influenced philosophers and theologians of all times.

waist-coateers Low-class prostitutes.

chambering Licentiousness.

Synopsis Philosophiae A reference to the writings of St Thomas Aquinas.

consumptive man with the doll's face... Even in a sentence or two, a fine example of how the unusual or the grotesque makes its impact upon Stephen's consciousness.

goatee A beard.

a priest-like face The priestly associations with Cranly indicate his role for Stephen – he hears his artistic confessions.

Ivory He is playing on and with words, but the associations once more go back to childhood – the Litany of the Blessed Virgin, tower of ivory, white hands, and so on.

India mittit ebur India sends ivory.

Contrahit orator 'The orator cuts down, the poet extends in song.' But Stephen is speaking of the laws of Latin verse, and his consciousness does not explain exactly what he means, it merely expresses.

in tanto discrimine In so great a turning point.

implere ollam denariorum To fill a pot of pennies.

Horace (65 BC–8 BC) Roman poet celebrated for his odes, satires and epistles.

John Duncan Inverarity ... William Malcolm Inverarity Probably just previous names written in.

vervain Small plant with blue, white or purple flowers.

like a dull stone set in a cumbrous ring A fine symbol to
reflect a weight of what Stephen considers to be dead learning.

the droll statue of the national poet of Ireland 'Droll' because
he is draped in a toga. The poet is Thomas Moore (1779–1852)
famous for *Lalla Rookh* and *Irish Melodies*, the latter having
some effect on the issue of Catholic Emancipation.

Firbolg ... Milesian The first is a reference to the original semi-
mythical inhabitants of Ireland, a dwarf-race; while the latter, in
complete contrast, were tall and attractive. They too were semi-
mythical.

Michael Cusack, the Gael A founder member of the Gaelic
Athletic Association.

the curfew was still a nightly fear The imposition of the curfew
would mean that no one would be allowed out after dusk. (See
section on *Political and religious background*.)

foreign legion of France Body of foreign volunteers in the
French army used in their colonies. It has severe discipline.

disremember Forget, but now out of use.

Buttevant On the main line north on the way to Limerick.

hurling match Traditional Irish game, something like
hockey.

stripped to his buff that day minding cool Naked to the waist,
keeping goal.

caman Stick.

within an aim's ace Very near. Joyce is intent on producing the
proverbial idiom and dialect that Davin would use.

a yoke Presumably a local word for 'conveyance'.

handsel A gift on entering upon new circumstances.

Wolfe Tone (1763–98) Irish patriot who formed the United
Irishmen, was captured by the English, condemned to death but
committed suicide in prison.

brake An open horse-drawn vehicle, with seats each side.

Buck Egan Fought a number of duels, and opposed the Union of
Ireland and England.

Burnchapel Whaley The hero of an Irish jingle, who 'walked to
Jerusalem for a bet'.

ephod Jewish priestly vestment.

prelatic High ecclesiastically.

hunkers The hams.

pulcra sunt quae 'Those things are beautiful which are pleasing
to the sight.'

Bonum est in quod 'The good is comprehended in that which is
wanted.'

Similiter atque senis The translation follows in the next line –
'like a staff in an old man's hand'.

Moher The cliffs in County Clare.

Epictetus The stoic philosopher of the 1st century whose
teachings are imbued with those of Christ.

detained in the full company of the saints Again a reference to
Newman's *The Glories of Mary*.

tundish A kind of funnel used in brewing.

as the elder may have turned on the prodigal See Luke 15,
11–32; the parable of the prodigal son.

seed and snake baptists Derogatory reference to nonconformist
minorities.

supralapsarian The doctrine that God's decrees preceded the
Fall and were therefore not due to it.

insufflation Breathing on a person as a rite of exorcism.

Per aspera ad astra Through hardship to the stars. Probably
a play on words, reference to *per ardua ad astra*: through
endeavour to the stars. (Ancient motto of the Mulvaney family.)

Kentish fire Prolonged volley of applause, or display of dissent.

Leopardstown The famous racecourse, not far from Dublin.

W. S. Gilbert (1836–1911) The writer of a number of popular
operas, among them *The Mikado* and *The Gondoliers*. They were
set to music by Sir Arthur Sullivan. The quotation is from a
song in *The Mikado*.

the cloister of Stephen's mind... These connected images
reflect the puritanical element in Stephen.

like a giraffe Fine image to indicate the 'jungle' of learning in
which Stephen finds himself – but it is not the kind of learning
on which he can feed.

platinoid An alloy of copper, zinc, platinum and tungsten.

a devil for his pound of flesh i.e. he is determined to have all
that he can get. Compare Antonio's bond with Shylock for the
pound of flesh which provides the basis of the main plot in
Shakespeare's *The Merchant of Venice*.

Closing time Moynihan is the wit of the class, comparing the
bell at the end of the lecture to the closing-bell in a pub.

Ego habeo 'I have.'

Quod 'What.'

Per pax universalis 'For universal peace.'

Credo ut vos Cranly is 'modernizing' his Latin. What he means
is that he knows that Stephen is a 'bloody liar' and that he can
tell from his face that he's in a bad mood.

Ready to shed the last drop... McCann is ready to die for
peace, to make a new world, to advocate temperance, and to
support votes for women.

A sugar! Appears to be Cranly's own word to indicate someone who should be despised.

Quis est in malo Stephen replies in the same kind of Latin as Cranly: 'Who's in a bad mood, you or I?'

the Tsar's rescript Nicholas II (1868–1918). Despite his peace circulars, the Bolshevik revolution saw his downfall and execution.

of Stead (1949–1912) Edition of the *Pall Mall Gazette*, involved in a trial for procuring a girl of thirteen and getting her taken to the continent in order to show what could be done.

Marx is only a bloody cod Karl Marx (1818–83) wrote *Das Kapital*, on which Socialist doctrine is largely based.

Socialism was founded ... Collins Temple is showing off. There is no basis for what he says.

He denounced priestcraft ... John Anthony Collins A continuation of Temple's showing off.

Lottie Collins lost her drawers... Lottie Collins (1866–1910), well known music-hall performer who came to fame through her song 'Ta-Ra-Ra-Boom-De-Ay'. The quotation here is an adaptation of two lines of the song, a parody in effect.

Pax super 'Peace over the globe' – and Cranly throws in the Latin 'bloody' too.

icon Image or statue, regarded as sacred.

Nos ad manum 'Let's go and play handball.'

pp. 182–206

Jean-Jacques Rousseau (1712–78) French philosopher and educationalist, but of irregular living habits.

super spottum On the spot.

go-by-the-wall Underhanded.

Long pace, fianna! A reference to the Fenian Society and its drilling in preparation for the taking of Ireland by force.

office of arms ... the tree of my family i.e. to look up his ancestry in the appropriate office.

I shall try to fly by those nets Note the image – Stephen will not be ensnared by nationalism, just as he was not ensnared by religion.

Ireland is the old sow that eats her farrow i.e. Ireland destroys her litter (her people).

eke The kind of archaism Cranly would use. It means 'also'.

yellow Lynch's substitute for 'bloody'.

the Venus of Praxiteles Praxiteles was a great Greek sculptor, born in Athens. The original marble statue of Aphrodite (Venus) was at Cnidus.

kinetic Due to motion.

Pulcra sunt quae See note p. 55.

stasis It appears to mean still, unmoving; the opposite of kinetic.

That seems to be a maze out of which ... Apt image for anyone called Dedalus, but perhaps it occurs to Stephen because he is escaping.

The Origin of Species The book by Darwin (1809–82), published in 1859, in which he put forward the law of natural selection which has dominated the study of evolution ever since.

Maundy Thursday i.e. the Thursday before Easter.

Pange lingua gloriosi 'Sing, O tongue glorious.'

Vexilla Regis 'Banners of the King.'

Impleta sunt ... a ligno Deus A reference to the songs of David, and to God 'reigning from the tree', perhaps a synonym for the cross.

plucked i.e. failed.

Goethe and Lessing Goethe (1749–1832) the German poet, philosopher and prose writer. Lessing (1729–81) German writer and critic whose *Laocoon* is referred to immediately afterwards by Donovan. It is a critical analysis of poetry and art.

for me and my mate Notice how the commonplace and the elevated are seen in contradistinction throughout these exchanges.

Ad pulcritudinem... Stephen appends his own translation, and the important words are 'wholeness, harmony, radiance'.

you win the cigar i.e. you win the prize. A cigar was a common prize at the time.

Shelley likened beautifully to a fading coal The reference is to Shelley's long essay on 'The Defence of Poetry'.

Luigi Galvani Italian physician (1737–98), a devout Catholic, from whom the term 'galvanism' is derived.

Mona Lisa By Leonardo da Vinci (Louvre, Paris). It is perhaps the most famous painting in the world.

Lessing ... should not i.e. in *Laocoon* (see note above).

stewing i.e. working hard.

Ego credo ut vita... 'I believe that the poor people's lives in Liverpool are simply atrocious, simply bloody atrocious.'

tarrying in clusters of diamonds Fine economical poetic effect.

Are you not weary of ardent ways The poem, in fragments and in its full complexity, has a running ambiguity, being at times apparently addressed to Ireland, to the Virgin Mary, to E–C–, perhaps even to poetry, the creative life. The *villanelle* has nineteen lines on two rhymes; and Stephen, with technical mastery, keeps exactly to the set form.

the victory chant of Agincourt The original was written in 1450.

Gherardino da Borgo San Donnino An austere Franciscan monk of the thirteenth century.

a church which was the scullery-maid of christendom Unvoiced though it is, it is certainly the most outspoken thought that Stephen has about the Catholic Church.

By Killarney's Lakes and Fells Traditional Irish air, widely popular.

the latticed ear of a priest i.e. at confession.

a priest of the eternal imagination... Here, and in the *villanelle*, there is some irony in the fact that Stephen, who has rejected Catholicism, should think in religious terms of his own imagination and function, and should write using the established religious symbols and phraseology.

making a cowl of the blanket Even this image, with its religious associations, underlines what has been said above. Think back to when the word 'cowl' was used of Emma as they went to the tram.

What birds were they? The whole of this sequence encloses a mystical experience, in which the birds symbolize Stephen's urge to travel into experience, but even as he wishes this he thinks, for instance, of his mother's 'sobs and reproaches'.

like threads of silken light unwound from whirring spools Superb poetic effect, but there is also a suggestion of a film, a picture, capturing the scene for later use, just as the memory stores an epiphany like this.

Cornelius Agrippa (1486–1535) Wrote of the occult sciences.

Swedenborg (1688–1772) A mystical thinker to whom the only real world was the spirit-world.

the curved stick of an augur The latter was a Roman official who foretold future events by omens derived from the actions of birds, among other things.

osier-woven Shoots of species of willow used in basketwork.

Thoth The Egyptian Mercury, inventor of arts and sciences, usually represented as having the body of a man and the head of an ibis.

Bend down your faces, Oona and Aleel This is from *The Countess Cathleen*, by W. B. Yeats, published in 1892 but not produced until 1899. It aroused much controversy.

A soft liquid joy This is the beginning of self-recognition – the augury of the birds, the swallows, whose departure symbolizes his own. The quotation from Yeats reinforces it; the associations are with the narrowness of his contemporaries and thus of Irish life.

A libel on Ireland This, and the phrases that follow, reflect the students' condemnation of *The Countess Cathleen*

A sudden swift hiss This signals the return to the present after the flashback to the theatre performance.

The Tablet Catholic weekly newspaper.

Our men retired in good order A parody of newspaper reportage of war.

Sir Walter Scott (1771–1832) The Scottish novelist, poet and critic, redressed an appalling financial disaster by writing the series of novels which began with *Waverley* (1814).

The Bride of Lammermoor By Scott, first published in 1819, and considered by some critics to be his best-constructed work.

The park trees were heavy with rain This superb paragraph is at first difficult to unravel, but close attention shows us that Stephen is pondering on the incestuous love of the dwarf they have just spoken to. Thus the embracing couple are the dwarf and his sister – but it all takes place in Stephen's imagination.

shrivelled mannikin i.e. the dwarf, little man.

the Bantry gang A group opposed to Parnell who largely came from Bantry.

pp. 207–28

riding a hack to spare the hunter Presumably riding a poor horse to save a good one; that is, doing the ordinary or commonplace as distinct from the attractive. Perhaps, acting with prudence or economy.

the Forsters Temple's usual camouflage for his own lack of real knowledge.

Giraldus Cambrensis (1147–1223) Ecclesiastic and author who left a very readable account of his times.

Pernobilis et pervetusta familia 'A very celebrated and old family.'

paulo post futurum The future-perfect, literally 'the state resulting from a future act'.

ballocks The word means 'testicles', and is here used as a form of self-denigration, the person who knows that he is of no account.

Dowland and Byrd and Nash The first two wrote music in the reign of James I (1603–25), while the third was the dramatist of the Elizabethan period, and wrote pamphlets of some significance too.

a slobbering Stuart A derogatory reference to James I.

the language of memory ambered wines Stephen works through a number of associations of music to the sordid realities – the licentious behaviour of the audiences.

A louse crawled over the nape Once again the sordid in the imagination leads him to the sordid he now experiences.

Cornelius à Lapide (1567–1637) A Jesuit writer.

sugan A rope of hay or straw.

limbo Region on the border of Hell where pre-Christian good men and unbaptized infants are confined.

Roscommon A county in Eire.

Siegfried An opera by Richard Wagner (1813–83).

jarvies Drivers of Irish cars.

her greeting to him under the porch Stephen is still smarting under the fact that E–C– had acknowledged Cranly but not him when they met.

I will not serve This, and Cranly's reply, show that they are aware of the association with Satan's words.

bright, agile, impassible ... subtle Stephen is being very sarcastic – he has deliberately chosen to use the words applied to the just after the Last Judgment. Cranly notes just how 'supersaturated' Stephen is in his rejected religion.

Pascal (1623–62) Distinguished French writer and thinker. His *Provincial Letters* were in defence of the Jansenists and against the Jesuits.

Aloysius Gonzaga (1569–91) Jesuit Saint.

Suarez (1548–1617) Jesuit religious writer.

Rosie O'Grady Popular song, having a wide music-hall currency at the time.

Mulier cantat 'This woman is singing.'

Et tu cum Jesu 'And you too were with Jesus the Galilean.' Stephen is obviously thinking of song in the church service.

proparoxytone With the acute accent on the last syllable but two.

And when we are married The last verse of 'Rosie O'Grady', it reflects conventional life, from which Stephen is turning away.

Juan Mariana de Talavera Sixteenth century Jesuit.

silence, exile, and cunning Ironic, for 'silence' to Stephen is verbal only in the sense that he will be using the written rather than the spoken word.

Yes, my child Cranly, although he opposes Stephen's heresy, has now heard his confession, and is imitating the voice of the priest.

coursing matches Pursuit of hares with greyhounds.

the precursor John the Baptist, with following references to his beheading ('severed head' and 'decollation'). The *fold* refers to the Jesuits.

Saint John at the Latin gate A reference to the feast day of May 6th celebrating St John the Evangelist's being spared.

Ghezzi One of Joyce's teachers.

Bruno the Nolan Burned as a heretic in Rome in 1600.

risotto An Italian dish of meat and rice.

Stephen's, that is, my green Where he has walked so often, by the University.

A quartet of them Obvious reference to the crucifixion, but ironically updated by Stephen.

I wonder if William Bond will die Poem of about 1802 by William Blake, the first line of which is 'I wonder whether the girls are mad'.

diorama Three-dimensional figures viewed through windows in representation of scenes.

William Ewart Gladstone Distinguished nineteenth century statesman (1809–98) and Liberal leader.

her brother All references to 'she' and 'her' from now on are to E–C–.

Lepidus The latter is one of the triumvirate in *Antony and Cleopatra*, and in Act 2, Scene 7, he engages Antony in talk of Egypt. Stephen virtually reproduces here lines 26 and 27 of that scene.

Tara The Hill of Tara was in ancient times the religious, political and cultural capital of Ireland; upon its summit are the coronation stone of the ancient kings, and a statue of St Patrick.

Michael Robartes remembers forgotten beauty The original title of a poem by W. B. Yeats (1865–1939).

I desire to press in my arms i.e. that which has not yet come into my experience.

Faintly, under the heavy night Notice the movement in this paragraph, perhaps anticipating the journey to come.

European and Asiatic papers please copy... A flippant reference to unimportant news items being often recorded in far away places.

I fear him i.e. because he typifies ignorant Ireland, what I might come to be like if I stay.

the spiritual-heroic refrigerating apparatus, invented and patented in all countries in Dante Alighieri The latter (1265–1321), the great poet of Italy who wrote the *Divine Comedy*. He idealized his love Beatrice in a series of poems, but she died and he married another. Stephen's reference satirically indicates the purity and chasteness of his love.

to forge in the smithy of my soul... Stephen appears to mean that he will create something from himself and Ireland that is *not* the 'created' conscience of religion and nationalism.

Old father Daedalus. See section on *Mythical background*.

Revision questions on Chapter 5

1 Describe any incident in this section which reveals the nature of Stephen's mind.

2 In what ways does Stephen view the present and the past?

3 Write brief character studies of any *two* of Stephen's friends or contemporaries.

The characters

Stephen

He would create proudly out of the freedom and power of his soul, as the great artificer whose name he bore, a living thing, a living thing, new and soaring and beautiful, impalpable, imperishable.

Stephen is the focus of all events and experiences in *A Portrait*, as the title indicates, and there are two basic ways of exploring his character. Firstly, there is the revelation of him through his own consciousness, and secondly there is the author's appraisal of him. Sometimes the two are so blended as to be virtually indistinguishable, and for the convenience of students reading this Study Aid Stephen's important personality or character traits are listed below. Throughout, Stephen is treated as Stephen and *not* as James Joyce, for there is nothing to be gained by confusing the author and his creation; to read for the autobiographical elements is tempting but fruitless, since we are judging *A Portrait* as a work of fiction. And since the length of *A Portrait* is the length of Stephen's life as far as Joyce takes it, the study of Stephen given here should be treated as an outline, with some areas perhaps shaded in more heavily than others. The thorough student may supplement it by investigating the text himself in order to establish other traits of character, or to compare his interpretation with mine. *A Portrait* is a complex novel, and within it Stephen has a complex mind. Consequently see what you, the reader, can find.

Above all else, Stephen is *sensitive*, and his senses are ever alert. There is early emphasis on his sense of smell (he prefers the smell of his mother to that of his father); his sense of taste (food is constantly mentioned, both at Clongowes and in the Dedalus home when Stephen is at University); his sense of touch (remember his wetting the bed, his being shouldered into the slimy square ditch, Eileen's hands); his hearing, particularly the sound of bat against ball in childhood from the far fields; and his sight. The last is most important, for the breaking of Stephen's glasses on the cinder-track means that he cannot read – or write – properly, and words are, and always will be, his mental food. The immediate and unjust result is that Stephen is caned by the Prefect of Studies. But his poor sight has, so to speak, compensations, for his inward sight, the eye of the imagination, is acutely developed, and in the latter stages of the novel his outward sight – of the clouds, of the sea, of birds – is linked with that heightened inward vision which assures him of his destiny. The child Stephen is father to the man Stephen, if we can use Wordsworth's definition of human maturity, for all that develops in Stephen later is consistent with what we know of his infancy and childhood.

His sensitivity in childhood takes a number of forms: he is *fearful* and *apprehensive* at Clongowes, something of the mother's boy who does not wish to be away from his home. He is *effeminate* and *withdrawn* at this stage, always keeping on the edge of a game if he can, rather than being involved in it; he lives in his own world rather than in that of the rough boys like Nasty Roche and Wells. He is *naive* and finds great difficulty in understanding the innuendo of his companions, and he is sensitive and *doubtful* of what is right (is it right to kiss your mother?) and already aware of differences in status (his father is not a magistrate). He is intensely *subjective* and *susceptible*, and these traits lead him to *introspection* and, of course, to the exercise of his *imagination*. His illness, during which he has a vision of Parnell's death, reflects his capacity for vivid and imaginative association, here heightened presumably by his temperature into a kind of delirium. That he is highy *intelligent*, and that this provides the basis for his intellectual development, we have no doubt; he is *competitive* in class at Clongowes, and his obsessions in later life are balanced by a high degree of intellectual and *rational* discipline.

For example, he works out his own artistic creed and, as he looks back over the forces which have shaped him in family, school, religion and literature, there comes to him that *decisive* concern to be done with the past and to strike out for himself. That singular mark of determination is present early on when, after being pandied, unseeing and racked with pain, he has the *courage* to go and see the Rector and make his lonely complaint of injustice. This action bears the stamp of the unusual boy who will become an unusual man. Stephen's stirrings against injustice become the later rejection of both narrow nationalism and narrow religious life. Both the early and the later actions require *integrity* and moral courage. In early life these marked a hesitant movement; in later years a visionary embrace.

The sensitive boy, having said Grace at the Christmas dinner, listens to the political and religious exchanges with apprehension and bewilderment, but later rejects both the worlds which they embody. That same boy moves through experiences of sensations to sensuality; from the naiveté of childhood (he doesn't know what 'smugging' is) to sexual awakening, to the first sexual encounter with the prostitute. This is followed, inevitably, by remorse and guilt, and these drive him away from the 'sins of the flesh' and into the arms of the spiritual lover, the Church. This progression, the consistency with which the evolution of Stephen's responses, changes, retrogressions and awakenings is handled, implies an intimate identification on the part of the author, but it also shows a feeling for artistic consonance. There is no flaw in the presentation of Stephen; he is *real*, whether in suffering or ecstasy, in solitary self-communion or in abrasive or light-hearted interaction with his fellows. We are *with* him, and we are *in* him, in the infirmary, at Christmas dinner, at the retreat listening to the hell-fire sermon, or walking through the streets, or suddenly encountering the dwarf. Joyce captures superbly the divisions between father and son, especially in the Cork sequence where Stephen becomes aware of his difference, his *isolation*, the fact that he can never be as his father hopes he will be.

Characteristically, this brings on a further feeling of guilt, and Stephen later tries hard to make up for what he is beginning to feel are his own inadequacies. With his prize money he buys food for the family and takes them out for a treat, seeing this as a symbol of conformity which they will appreciate. But between his father's fluent, nostalgic, pub bonhomie, his mother's hardening religiosity and the descending scale of family finances, falls the clear light of escape. Before it irradiates Stephen with the power of the future, he passes through an agonizing struggle and an agonizing temptation.

That temptation is to go to the extreme of conformity in the religious sense, and enter the priesthood. From Clongowes to the Jesuit school at Belvedere – leaving aside social status – is a movement of degree. Stephen's mind and his body draw him towards the sensual and the intellectual, independent of spiritual gratifications. But the grasp of the religion in which he has been reared, sometimes nurtured, sometimes knocked, is tyrannical enough to turn his nature back on itself. The result is that after the sermons he takes a kind of *joy in self-abasement, a delight in renunciation*; he rejects the appetites of the flesh, even sitting, or standing in one position of discomfort to test his will. The pleasures are the pleasures of control, of something achieved. Stephen's zest for the whole area of such sacrifice is a spiritual one.

For a time this spiritual diet is sufficient sustenance for Stephen. Yet the little boy who pondered on the attractions of words, considered their associations and meanings, now finds himself pondering on *the* word, the word of God. Stephen's questioning spirit and, above all, the pictures and music of his imagination, are not stilled by observance, ritual or dogma. The clear air of enquiry, the broad expanse of freedom from dogmatic, domestic or national restraint, is his to explore. From little-boy-outsider to intelligent-radical-cum-sceptical young man is but a short step and Stephen, after his initial rejection of the priestly vocation, takes it.

This is not to say that his torments are over, for he must still resolve the attractions of the flesh, the temptation towards E–C– and the domestic pressures, and he must still 'fashion' (he is an 'artificer') his artistic creed. His senses and his mind, the twin centres of his conscious (and subconscious) activity, are alert to the struggle. His recollection of the phrase 'A day of dappled seaborne clouds', his mystical – strongly visual and sensual – appraisal of the girl in midstream ('Her image had passed into his soul for ever and no word had broken the holy silence of his ecstasy'), and his rapture at this *sudden finding of himself* all reflect his ardent capacity for experience and imaginative identification. Strangely, 'ardent' is the word he plays on throughout the *villanelle* he writes for E–C–.

From now on Stephen is set on a voyage of dedication and discovery; he traces the intellectual and emotive influences of his life – Newman, Aristotle, Aquinas, the 'dainty songs' of the Elizabethans – and, at the University, feels disgust and repugnance for the life he is leading. Stephen swings always on the pendulum of *self-distrust*, shame and at the same time *frustration* at the physical and mental trappings of his lot. As he walks in Dublin the denial of his country, of its stifling nationalism and its priest-ridden compulsion, wells up within him. His conversation with the Dean and his attendance at lectures help to focus his spirit and to confirm in him his sense of difference and isolation. Exchanges with his fellow students underline this central aspect of his self-evaluation. His rational assessment of himself, of religion, of life, is expressed in his conversations with Lynch, as is indeed his full definition of the artist and the artist's function.

But he is still aware of E–C–, and has erotic and poetic fantasies about her, writes the *villanelle*, and moves through sensations, responses, associations of words and imagination, towards the decision, the fulfilment which his cramped poverty, intellectual and physical, cannot give him. From lust for E–C– and the sordid present ('A louse crawled over the nape of his neck') he must escape, and although Cranly reasons with him about his attitude towards religion, his mind is set:

Away then: it is time to go. A voice spoke softly to Stephen's lonely heart, bidding him go and telling him that his friendship was coming to an end. (*Chapter 5*, p.221).

He follows the dictates of his heart, his mind, his imagination. His diary entries reflect his purpose, a purpose that is at once challenge and escape. He writes, 'I desire to press in my arms the loveliness which has not yet come into the world'. The images – Stephen is always concerned with words – link the 'white arms' of sensuality with the 'white arms of roads' that will take him away. The step is into the unknown, and Stephen's decision carries perhaps for his own character an overtone of irony. His other steps have been towards rejection and frustration. Will this one be so too?

In the preceding paragraphs the main facets of Stephen's character are described but, to coin Tennyson's words, they are 'given in outline and no more'. The reason is obvious, for every moment of the novel belongs to Stephen, from the inward monologue to his outward contributions to speech and events. And since the texture of the novel is so closely woven, with every stitch an implication, you, the reader, are advised to look closely at the *crises* of Stephen's existence in order to supplement or extend the deductions given above. Explore the degrees of his sensitivity, the turns of his imagination, the quality of his rational pronouncements, and look closely too at those sections of this Study Aid which deal with *Style* and *Textual notes*, for in them you find comments on the language Joyce uses to define his hero's essential nature.

Mr Dedalus

A medical student, an oarsman, a tenor, an amateur actor, a shouting politician, a small landlord, a small investor, a drinker, a good fellow, a story-teller, somebody's secretary, something in a distillery, a taxgatherer, a bankrupt and at present a praiser of his own past.

The above recital by Stephen about his father, Simon Dedalus, even if we allow for the irony (it is an echo of an earlier statement), encompasses the one word, failure. The material descent of Mr Dedalus is reflected in the moral descent of Stephen, Blackrock being equated with freedom and illusion, while Dublin is accompanied by domestic (and inward) degradation for the growing boy. Mr Dedalus appears much larger than life in the Christmas dinner scene, thus providing further evidence of Joyce's ability to present the adult world through the sensations of a child. Our glimpses of Simon before that are sparse; 'he had a hairy face, wears a monocle' (perhaps indicative of affectation), and when Stephen goes to Clongowes tells him 'never to peach on a fellow'. In his delirium in the infirmary Stephen imagines that his father is a marshal, 'higher than a magistrate', but we soon form the impression that Mr Dedalus is feckless, improvident, a hail-fellow-well-met but with a tendency to irresponsible action which he cannot curb. He is vain, proud of his appearance, as we see when he looks at himself in the pierglass; he can be ironic ('I wonder if there's any likelihood of dinner this evening'), he drinks steadily, and is a fine mimic (witness his impersonation of the hotel-keeper). He is tolerant of Stephen as a child, and has a sense of propriety as we see when he has Stephen say grace. He is also sentimental – he cries when he sees Stephen dressed for mass because 'He was thinking of his own father'.

Always he is to indulge this nostalgia, filial and general, but he is provocative to Dante, telling a joke against the priests; this really sparks off the row over the rejection of Parnell by the Church. This row waxes fast and furious, observed by the bewildered and impressionable Stephen. Once or twice Simon seems to be turning his back on direct provocation, but he is the kind of man who can't resist the opportunity to fan the flames of differences, and his reference to the 'pope's nose', innocent in another context, is fuel to this. It leads to a silence during which he is moved to say, 'Well, my Christmas dinner has been spoiled, anyhow'. In the altercation which follows he shows himself to be both loud and coarse, and later he urges Mr Casey to tell a story which he knows will offend Dante. The prospect of this puts him in a good humour again, and he tears off morsels of meat with relish. His role, briefly but importunately, is to see that Mr Casey continues this story to its insulting conclusion. When it is over he refers to Ireland as a 'priest-ridden Godforsaken race!', and after the final screaming exit of Dante, Stephen looks up at his father and sees that his 'eyes were full of tears'. The combination of drink, maudlin nostalgia and intense nationalism, causes Mr Dedalus to react in this way.

This scene marks his only physical appearance in Chapter 1, but in Chapter 2 he reappears, for at this stage the family is at Blackrock, and often on Sundays Mr Dedalus walks ten or twelve miles with Stephen and Uncle Charles. By now Stephen is aware in a vague way that his father is in difficulties, and when they move to Dublin Mr Dedalus finally asserts himself ('There's a crack of the whip left in me yet'). Mr Dedalus arranges for Stephen to go to Belvedere, and once again displays his talent for imitation by doing 'the mincing, nasal tone of the provincial' (the Rector) who has told him the story of Stephen's complaint against Father Dolan for pandying him unjustly. For Simon, it is a story to recount to friends and acquaintances in the city bars.

Stephen, however, is beginning to feel a certain shame, and on the night of the Whitsuntide play Heron reports seeing Mr Dedalus escorting E–C– 'staring at her through that eyeglass of his for all he was worth'. This may imply that he thinks of himself as a ladies' man but Stephen, embarrassed, gets away from his father as quickly as he can after the play. When they go to Cork together, Simon Dedalus's main characteristics are strongly imprinted on the reader's mind; he constantly *recurs* to the past ('a tale broken by sighs or draughts from his pocket flask') but for Stephen the present is the be-all and end-all ('his father's property was going to be sold by auction'). Mr

Dedalus is in good voice, enjoys identifying his own initials cut in a desk in the anatomy theatre of Queen's College, and then treats Stephen to a recital of his youth and subsequent career, words which remain in Stephen's memory and are used by him with telling irony – the same words which are quoted at the head of this section on Mr Dedalus. This is his father's longest speech, and the main point of it is that Stephen should 'mix with gentlemen ... fellows of the right kidney ... bloody good honest Irishmen'. There is always a note of nostalgia and pride, particularly in *his own father*, which makes Mr Dedalus's 'voice break into a laugh which was almost a sob'. He drinks heavily, to Stephen's shame, flirts with the barmaids and exults in others' recollections of his prowess with women.

After Stephen's prize, and the initial spending involved Mr Dedalus fades from the action; his last words are shouted down from the stairs ('Is your lazy bitch of a brother gone out yet?'). Poverty has reduced him – large, loud, happy in his cups, incapable of understanding his son's nature – and we see him there recumbent, probably from a hangover. And perhaps we think, too, that despite his descent, he could still cut something of a dash in any level of society.

Mrs Dedalus

His mother had a nicer smell than his father. She played on the piano the sailor's hornpipe for him to dance.

Mrs Dedalus, central to Stephen's early existence, appears but fitfully in the action of the novel. She is protective towards Stephen (her eldest), telling him 'not to speak with the rough boys in the college'. Significantly, when he is ill Stephen thinks of writing to his mother but at the Christmas dinner, which is dominated by discussion of Parnell and the Church, Mrs Dedalus's role is simply that of organizer and peace-maker ('for pity sake, let us have no political discussion on this day of all days in the year'). Her failure is apparent, and she eats little, reprimanding her husband for speaking the way he does before Stephen. Mrs Dedalus is clearly a woman of her time, subordinate, domestic, fearful of the encroachment of the outside world ('not even for one day in the year ... can we be free from these dreadful disputes').

Later, when they move from Blackrock to Dublin, she is 'red-eyed' as she sits in the railway carriage with Stephen, but pleased when Mr Dedalus arranges for Stephen to go to Belvedere. When her son spends his money on treating them, Mrs Dedalus, ever mindful of poverty, begs to eat in 'Some place that's not too dear ... Some quiet place' mindful, too, perhaps, of their loss of status. We can imagine this feeling heightened later when the family has to make do with 'small glass jars and jampots which did service for teacups'. She is 'hostile to the idea' of Stephen going to the University, and Stephen is aware of the 'first noiseless sundering of their lives' as he watches her religious faith 'ageing and strenthening in her eyes'. We might add that this faith is all she has left, for her last appearance in the novel shows her nagging her wayward son who is late for his lecture. The domestic conditions now are hopelessly degraded, and she observes that 'it's a poor case ... when a university student is so dirty that his mother has to wash him'. She tells him that the University has changed him; her presence remains a barrier to Stephen, and he confides in Cranly that he has had an 'unpleasant quarrel' with his mother about religion, more particularly because she wishes him 'to make my Easter duty'. She is a woman overburdened by the onset of poverty and the birth over the years of nine or ten children of whom, says Stephen, 'Some died'. As Stephen prepares for his final leavetaking of his family, his mother prays that he will finally learn 'what the heart is and what it feels'.

Uncle Charles

a hale old man with a well-tanned skin, rugged features and white side whiskers.

Stephen's uncle Charles is 'older than Dante' but thinks, like Mr Dedalus, that she is 'a clever woman and a wellread woman'. He remains neutral in the Church versus Parnell argument. Before it begins he sits 'far away, in the shadow of the window'. Mr Dedalus defers to him as the oldest member of the family, serves him and asks him if the bird is tender. Uncle Charles's mouth is then too full, but later it is empty enough for him to try to calm things down. He thinks it bad that there should be too much talk in front of Stephen. Later all he can do is to sway his head 'to and fro', and all he can say is 'A bad business! A bad business!' At Blackrock, though, he emerges as much more of a character, smoking 'black twist' of such a strong nature that Simon urges him to enjoy it 'in a little outhouse at the end of the garden'. This he does urbanely, considering that it will be 'more salubrious', the tobacco of his choice being 'cool and mollifying'. He is a clean old man, likes singing, and is Stephen's constant companion in the first part of the summer at Blackrock. He sends Stephen on errands, but rewards him generously with, for example, grapes and American apples. He enjoys talking to Mike Flynn about athletics and politics, and is a pious old man, visiting the chapel and praying, and sprinkling Stephen lightly with water from the font. His prayers cause Stephen to ponder that he may be concerned with 'the grace of a happy death or perhaps he prayed that God might send him back a part of the big fortune he had squandered in Cork'. Uncle Charles is a 'nimble walker' and takes part in the Sunday constitutional. But when the family moves to Dublin his age and infirmity set in, and he is 'grown so witless' that he cannot be sent on errands any more. His kindness to Stephen is much appreciated by the boy, and it is this kindness that we remember as his chief quality. His image, however, fades from Stephen's memory as he and his father go to Cork for the auction.

Dante

Dante had ripped the green velvet back off the brush that was for Parnell one day with her scissors and had told him that Parnell was a bad man.

Mrs Riordan, the 'aunty' who became 'Dante' in a childish attempt to pronounce the word, is a strongly religious woman who gives Stephen his first lessons. She is particularly keen on geography, which she manages to tie in with her religion by mentioning a place where, for example, St Francis Xavier stopped. In Stephen's earliest recollections she is a supporter of Davitt *and* Parnell (see the section on *Political and religious background*). She suffers from heartburn, is supposed to be a clever and educated woman who occasionally gives Stephen a cachou, and is a fervent Irish Catholic who supports the Church's condemnation of Parnell. In Stephen's vision of the death of the great Irish leader, Dante is not wailing but is walking 'proudly and silently' past the kneeling people.

The political argument owes much to the baiting of Mr Dedalus and Mr Casey. Dante is unequivocal in her defence of the Church, and in fact advances the classical argument that 'It is a question of public morality. A priest would not be a priest if he did not tell his flock what is right and what is wrong'. She considers that Parnell was a 'public sinner', and she responds just as strongly to the attack on the 'Lord's anointed'. According to Simon Dedalus, Dante is a 'spoiled nun', and among other things she does not like Stephen to play with Eileen, who is a Protestant. But Stephen remembers when she was *for* Parnell, and how she had hit a gentleman on the head with her umbrella because he had 'taken off his hat when the band played "God save the Queen"'. Dante's assertions that 'The priests were always the true friends of Ireland' provokes the final round of the argument in which Mr Casey demands 'No God for Ireland', and Dante exits screaming that 'We crushed him to death'. She takes no further part in the action. Obviously the Dedaluses' means have become severly circumscribed, and Dante could hardly be paid for her teaching. One wonders too if, after this scene, she wouldn't depart from choice anyway.

Mr Casey

Mr Casey had told him that he had got those three cramped fingers making a birthday present for Queen Victoria.

Based on the character of John Kelly, who was imprisoned on several occasions and suffered damage to his fingers, Mr Casey is a sentimental, somewhat aggressive but humorous Parnellite. One can see what he has in common with Mr Dedalus – a zest for talk and reminiscence, and a certain coarseness which is apparent in his pro-Parnell anecdote. This, we remember, ends with his spitting in the eye of the woman agitator which is the action which incenses Dante, who becomes in effect the kind of woman Mr Casey has just damned. The effect of the scene is that Mr Casey becomes very maudlin over Parnell – 'My dead king!' – and he sobs 'loudly and bitterly'. He has a loud and persuasive way of talking, and we can readily imagine him making speeches from a wagonette. There is something poignant about him, despite the bravado of his speech, his earnest irony at the expense of the Church, and his coarse humour. Perhaps it is because he is the genuine patriot, and his 'sob of pain' is from the heart.

Heron

A shock of pale hair lay on the forehead like a ruffled crest.

Perhaps the most vivid of the Belvedere characters, Heron does much loafing about, smoking and casual bullying. He first appears on the night of the Whitsuntide play, and he calls Stephen in a 'high throaty voice', bowing in mock deference, and poking the ground with his cane. He wants Stephen to impersonate the Rector's speech in the play, and after his own incompetent mimicry, he refers sarcastically to Stephen as a 'model youth'. He also calls him a 'sly dog' because he has seen Mr Dedalus with a girl who is 'ripping'. Jealous of Stephen's 'saintly' image, he strikes him lightly with his cane (an affectation of foppishness) and this recalls to Stephen's mind the other occasion when Heron figured prominently in his life. This had been some time before in his career at Belvedere, when Heron and his friends Boland and Nash baited Stephen on their chosen ground of literature. Stephen is well aware of their mockery, but vows to keep silent, a vow he is forced to break when Tennyson is elevated above his idol, Byron. Stephen, a 'heretic', has his legs cut by Heron's cane, and is beaten by his tormentors, but he bears no malice. Heron always has someone with him – at the Whitsuntide play it is the execrable Wallis. He uses the affectation of slang freely ('you're taking a part of his bally old play'), and is obviously meant to stand in contradistinction to Stephen. He is a bully and a *pretence* rebel, mocking but never being found out. Stephen, on the other hand, is the real rebel, the boy of integrity standing against the establishment.

Other characters at Clongowes and Belvedere

These are all minor in the sense that they pass in and out of Stephen's life. *Wells* is almost a pale anticipation of Heron, a bully who shoulders Stephen into the square ditch 'because he would not swop his little snuffbox for Wells' seasoned hacking chestnut, the conqueror of forty'. He also baits Stephen about kissing his mother, but apologizes to Stephen when he finds out that he is ill. *Brother Michael* in the infirmary talks in clichés ('You'll get your walking papers in the morning when the doctor comes'), but is not without a certain kindness. *Athy* tries hard to keep Stephen's spirits up with his jokes, and later he tells some of the fellows how a group of boys have been caught 'smugging' in the 'square'. *Mr Harford*, one of the masters, 'was very decent and never got into a wax'. *Father Arnall*, however, does, and has Fleming kneel out in front of the class because of the disgusting state of his themebook. The Prefect of Studies, *Father Dolan*, is a caricature: he is the arbitrary punishment man, who pandies Stephen unjustly, and his loud bullying tones and rhetorical questions (he doesn't really listen to the answers, and can twist them if he does) plus the ritualistic threats, are all instances of the power of the establishment in such a school and of the effects it can have. To be fair, he is more than balanced by the kindness and understanding of the *Rector* who, without in any way undermining his own position, sees that the humane – and diplomatic – way to deal with Stephen's complaint is to take due note of it. The irony is, of course, that Father Dolan's habits of authority will not be changed; they may even be more deviously applied.

In Blackrock, Stephen is put through his training sessions by *Mike Flynn*. The latter is a fine example of Joyce's economic style, for he is brought alive, visually at least, by one or two deft touches, and remains in our mind although we do not meet him again. We remember his 'flabby stubble-covered face' and the 'mild lustreless blue eyes'. *Aubrey Mills* and Stephen found a 'gang of adventurers', and Aubrey carried 'a whistle dangling from his buttonhole and a bicycle lamp attached to his belt', but unfortunately he has to go to school and is only free in the evenings.

Fine, ironic caricature is seen in Joyce's presentation of the *Director* who 'smiled, slowly dangling and looping the cord of the other blind'. Paradoxically, the gesture carries a symbolic inference – Stephen may be caught and thus enter the order, and indeed this is the prelude to the discussion of Stephen's 'vocation'. The Director does not come alive as a character, but his presence and the persuasive nature of his appeal are insidious, urbane, balanced. What he does not know, of course, is that it awakens in Stephen 'an instinct subtle and hostile', which 'armed him against acquiescence'. It is a further example of Joyce's irony that the preacher of the hell-fire sermon does *not* come alive through his words; however, impassioned they are, they are presented as the stereotype of spiritual persuasion, and consequently the man behind them is not seen, only heard.

Students at the university

McCann is a 'squat figure in a shooting jacket and breeches and with a fair goatee', and he tries to make Stephen more sociable. It is McCann who moves among the students collecting signatures for the testimonial to the Tsar, and he has a bantering exchange with Stephen. It becomes more serious when Stephen refuses to sign, and McCann accuses him of being reactionary. *Cranly* is early confided in by Stephen, and has a 'priestlike face, priestlike in its pallor', and he receives all Stephen's confidences with a 'listening silence'. He also has 'dark womanish eyes', often speaks in Latin or quotes it, and some of his remarks are tinged with bitterness. He is fond of commenting on others, more particularly on their shortcomings, and has quite a row with Temple. He has a skirmish, this time physical, with Lynch. He is kind to the dwarf, getting him to voice his admiration for Scott, but later follows Stephen; he is, as always, picking his teeth. E–C– bows to Cranly, who has given much evidence of being depressed, and Stephen wonders if she is responsible for his friend's 'listless silence, his harsh comments, the sudden intrusions of rude speech'. They walk on, with Cranly, whose habits are none of the best, eating a fig. After he has chased Temple, Stephen tells him his troubles, and particularly of his quarrel with his mother over religion. For a moment the two friends are drawn closely together again. Stephen forces Cranly to reject another fig, and they talk about religion, Cranly shifting his ground as he reasons with Stephen. When Stephen declares his creed, Cranly 'laughed almost slyly and pressed Stephen's arm with an elder's affection'. Stephen realizes that he has 'confessed' to his friend, whose own humour is equal to the occasion as he reveals when he calls him 'my child'. Stephen senses that Cranly has, however, 'spoken of himself, of his own loneliness which he feared'. There is much more to him than appears. He is obviously intelligent, hides behind his phrases and little outbursts of aggression, but lacks the will-power to do anything positive about himself and his emotional and intellectual needs. Stephen suspects him of being interested in E–C–, for he was 'invited there by her brother'. Stephen's diary entry perhaps sums Cranly up: 'Hence Cranly's despair of soul: the child of exhausted loins'.

Moynihan has a 'snoutish face' and a certain animal wit to go with it, what Stephen defines in his own mind as a 'rude humour'. He is quite a mimic, a clown who uses lectures to convey his cheeky flouting of authority and his satirical appraisal of his fellow students. He is particularly good on McCann ('Ready to shed the last drop. Brand new world. No stimulants and votes for the bitches'). He has obviously upset Cranly, but he has a certain quickness of response, so that when Temple refers to John Anthony Collins in a rather pedantic way, Moynihan caps it with a remark about Lottie Collins and the quotation from the parody of a music hall song. *Temple* is pretentious, constantly interjecting remarks, speaking importantly, and is considered by Cranly to be a 'go-by-the-wall'. His one redeeming feature is that he thinks that Stephen has 'an individual mind'.

Lynch is more important, since Stephen gives much of his time to talking to him. He laughs 'pitched in a high key . . . like the whinny of an elephant'. He swears 'in yellow'. He has told Stephen that as a boy 'in that charming carmelite school' he ate 'pieces of dried cowdung'. Stephen observes him closely, thinks him reptilian, yet sees in his eyes 'the window of a shrivelled soul, poignant and selfembittered'. Stephen develops in conversation with Lynch his aesthetic philosophy; Lynch is critical and witty, and there is one glorious moment of comedy when a heavy dray passes and covers the end of

Stephen's speech with its noise. Stephen then proceeds to define *integritas*, *consonantia* and *claritas*, definitions accompanied by a satirical commentary for Lynch. The latter is bitter about his poverty though, and speaks harshly of 'that yellow pancakeeating excrement' getting a good job when he can't. But perhaps his wittiest retort comes when he follows Stephen's self-conscious definition of the artist, 'invisible, refined out of existence, indifferent, paring his fingernails' with 'Trying to refine them also out of existence'. He has a certain resilience and individuality, and is far from being merely caricature.

Davin, the peasant student, nephew of the famous athlete Matt Davin, has worshipped 'the sorrowful legend of Ireland'. Despite this and Stephen's own mockery of it, Stephen feels some real affection for him. Davin can 'get through' to Stephen, and tells simply the story of his encounter with the peasant woman who invites him to stay the night. Stephen is 'won over to sympathy by the speaker's simple accent'. First of all Davin tells of the hurling match and then of the woman and how, in his shyness and embarrassment, he 'went on his way again, all in a fever'. The story imbeds itself in Stephen's imagination, and is almost as significant as his silent meeting with the girl paddling in midstream. Davin ('little tame goose') signs the testimonial to the Tsar, and calls Stephen a 'born sneerer', urging him to be 'one of us' and to 'learn Irish'. He considers himself 'a simple person', and tells him how much he suffered when Stephen told him 'those things'. He puts the Irish case strongly but simply when he asserts 'Ireland first, Stevie. You can be a poet or a mystic after'. He is sad when Stephen retorts 'Ireland is the old sow that eats her farrow', but soon loses himself in disputes over the game in which he is involved.

Other students – momentarily captured in idiosyncratic or casual exchange – like *Glynn, Dixon, McAlister* and *Goggins*, do not merit close attention. The *dwarfish man* with his love of Sir Walter Scott also registers, as does the *Dean*. With the latter Stephen debates 'the creation of the beautiful', but he has 'pale loveless eyes' and is really 'a poor Englishman in Ireland'. He cannot really respond with any degree of life to the cut and thrust of the debate, and Stephen outclasses him in terms of words and their associations. Even if we allow for Stephen's prejudice at this stage in his life, we feel the negation of the Dean and share Stephen's sense of a 'desolating pity' for him.

Style

Joyce is an innovatory stylist, adapting the conventional techniques of English fiction, extending them by coinages both individual and associative, and charging his language with the kind of expansive illuminations which are often to be found in poetry. In fact *A Portrait* is imbued with poetry, and those who think of Joyce as being too cerebral might look at the imagery of birds and nature which runs throughout the novel. It is platitude to say that Joyce's primary interest, like Stephen's, is in words, but it must be said if only to make the reader aware that he in turn should read by association and suggestion, and try to respond to the nuances of words and their echoic effects.

Stephen ponders early on the word 'belt'. Later he considers, in his dialogue with the Dean, the use of words in their different contexts, whether it be the market place or the literary tradition, and he uses the word 'detained' in a sentence from Newman as well as in its commonly understood form. Both these examples indicate Stephen's, and Joyce's, verbal tastes, a kind of etymological-pun-consciousness which the reader should be prepared to accept as one of the basic elements of the style. In addition, Joyce is very fond of running words together, disclaiming the hyphen as in, for instance, his 'fellowstudents' ruder humour'. Stephen is very sensitive to the *difference* of words, noting that '*home, Christ, ale, master*' mean one thing to him and another thing to the dean. Sometimes, he says, his 'soul frets in the shadow of his language'.

Joyce is a user of the senses, particularly of sight and sound. For Stephen, to remember 'the white look of the lavatory made him feel cold and then hot', while the gas 'made a light noise like a little song'. Colour, too, is very important, for the red and the green motif, with its associations of patriotism, of blood shed on the Emerald Isle, recurs throughout the book.

On the first page Stephen sings his song 'the wild rose blossoms/On the little green place', slurring and lisping it sleepily to 'the green wothe botheth'. In extension of this, there is the holly and the ivy at home, while Dante has a brush with a maroon velvet back, and one with a green velvet back, and Stephen colours the earth green and the clouds maroon in his geography book. Sound also bulks largely in the experiences of the little boy. The noise in the refectory 'made a roar like a train at night'. Linked with this is the repetition of hot and cold, with the sheets initially cold and then hot in bed. Frequently the repetition of sense responses creates the mood of a character, and Stephen is particularly sensitive, or vulnerable, in this respect. This saturation with words is both atmospheric and symbolic; even the sentences in Doctor Cornwell's spelling book, with the half-puns of Abbey, Abbots, Canker, Cancer, the linking of spirituality and disease (and Stephen is to experience both, almost as one) show the extent of Joyce's feeling for language.

This feeling is seen on another level in the songs and poems which occur throughout the book, from that of the 'wild rose' onwards. There is the song about the bell where the words are, for Stephen, 'beautiful and sad, like music', and there is of course the *villanelle*, written to E–C– (and perhaps to Ireland, and perhaps even to the Virgin Mary as epitomizing the Catholic Church). Song is very important for Joyce (who had a good voice) and also for Mr Dedalus. If one thinks of his song (the first verse of which ends with 'So I'll go to/ Amerikay') one sees again the depth at which Joyce works, for the words anticipate Stephen's decision to leave and seek his own (artistic) fortune elsewhere. The basic verbal style of *A Portrait* has embedded in it poems, songs and quotations, thus creating imaginative chains of association, a technique similar to that used by T. S. Eliot in *The Waste Land* (1922).

Joyce also uses a form of parody, and here so cleverly imitative that it is indistinguishable from the real thing. The best example in *A Portrait* is to be found in the sermons. The preacher's tone, the rhetorical twists and turns, show what a fine ear Joyce had for the cadences and rhythms of mannered, rehearsed, calculated delivery. For example:

No. You would not. You flouted the ministers of holy religion, you turned your back on the confessional, you wallowed deeper and deeper in the mire of sin. God appealed to you, threatened you, entreated you to return to Him. O what shame, what misery! The ruler of the universe entreated you, a creature of clay, to love Him Who made you and to keep His law. (*Chapter 3*, p.19)

What is so brilliant about this writing is the subtle distortion which mocks it from within. The rhetoric is empty, hollow, predictable, so that the mockery pervades the speaker's intention *and* the listener's (or reader's) susceptibility. This element of *irony*, present in Joyce's conception of Stephen as well, gives *A Portrait* that additional suggestion of ambiguity which is one of the marks of great writing.

Whose side is Joyce on? The answer is, of course, that he is not on any side but on all sides, perhaps looking back at states of mind or emotion which he knew, and presenting both their seriousness and their ridiculousness at the same time. In other words, there is an *ambivalence* about his style which has misled critics into crediting Joyce with intentions which are not relevant to our consideration of the finished work. Thus Wayne C. Booth can write (in *The Rhetoric of Fiction*) that 'Joyce was always a bit uncertain about his attitude towards Stephen'. Isn't it rather that the attitudes of Stephen are uncertain, and that the various styles of writing so intimately concerned with him reflect response, vacillation, change and decision? John Gross seems much nearer the truth when he says, 'The portrait of the artist turns out to be the dissection of the second-rate aesthete', because Joyce is sufficiently astute *not* to comment either on his hero's practices or on his decision. Thus the *villanelle* is written in a style fitting to that of a young man passing through a particular experience; we are not asked to judge it as poetry, though we may suspect that Joyce is smiling in his sleeve. The creed of the artist is defined by Stephen, but no comment is offered on the validity of the definition.

In Joyce, style is intimately identified with character and with mood. We have looked at the extract from the sermon, and perhaps we could do well to look at what J. S. Atherton speaks of when Stephen's 'romantic fantasies culminate ironically in a visit to a prostitute which is described in Paterian prose'. This apt comparison (for Stephen 'stretched out his arms in the street to hold fast the frail swooning form that eluded him and incited him') is some indication of Joyce's stylistic versatility. He has a number of styles, sounding boards of the mood or emotions of his hero. Joyce's own word mastery, and his wide reading, inform *A Portrait* with the irridescence of the literary life as well as the reality of experience.

This reality of experience is markedly present. Consider Stephen on a visit to Cork with his father, Stephen in the lecture theatre with his fellows, Stephen in the infirmary with Athy – all these are *realistic* scenes because the dialogue, the comment, the reactions from Stephen's consciousness are all immediate and credible. Both ear and eye are right; Joyce has a zest for detail, and nowhere is this more apparent than in the domestic detail which is sometimes given a symbolic weight. Here is Stephen after he has treated his family and the good intentions have burned away:

The pot of pink enamel paint gave out and the wainscot of his bedroom remained with its unfinished and illplastered coat. (*Chapter 2*, p.90)

This is a simple statement, but it also symbolizes the uncertainty of Stephen's life, his lack of will and self-knowledge at this stage, his inability to finish anything, either with his family or in his imaginative, artistic life. Joyce's use of symbol is widespread throughout the novel. The reader who has looked at the section of this Study Aid on *Mythical background* will recall the paragraphs on Daedalus, and certainly the idea of flight, the bird imagery, Stephen's contemplation of the birds from the library steps ('He watched their flight; bird after bird, a dark flash, a swerve, a flutter of wings') all anticipate his own final 'taking off', his questing and questioning mind, and the flights of his imagination.

This is just one example of the literal descriptions or comparisons carrying overtones of association. The symbolic mode is Joyce's natural extension of his text, with the result that some critics have seen Stephen, for example, as Daedalus, Icarus, Christ, or even Satan, while Cranly's relationship to him has been compared to that of John the Baptist with Christ.

Then we come to the most notable facets of Joyce's style in *A Portrait*. The first has been much defined and considered; Wayne C. Booth's statement (again in *The Rhetoric of Fiction*) almost conveys the quintessential Joycean intention. He describes what Joyce himself called an *epiphany* as 'a peculiar revelation of the inner reality of an experience, accompanied with great elation, as in a mystical religious experience'. We can stop here and consider the 'peculiar revelation', the 'elation' and the 'mystical experience' in relation to Stephen. The outstanding epiphany is with the girl in midstream, where the actual experience is transformed by the unique insight of the imagination. Here symbol and epiphany merge, and indeed one is tempted to say that an epiphany is an extended symbol:

She seemed like one whom magic had changed into the likeness of a strange and beautiful seabird. Her long slender bare legs were delicate as a crane's ... the white fringes of her drawers were like featherings of soft white down. Her slateblue skirts ... dovetailed behind her. Her bosom was as a bird's ... the breast of some darkplumaged dove. (*Chapter 4*, pp.155–6)

Thus far the symbolic association is clear – but Stephen's soul feels 'an outburst of profane joy ... Her image had passed into his soul for ever and no word had broken the holy silence of his ecstasy'. The removal to Dublin is associated with a cluster of three epiphanies: the first in his aunt's house, the second in the narrow breakfast room, the third at and after the children's party at Harold's Cross. And here we must quarrel with Professor Booth's word 'elated', for these experiences (epiphany literally means 'showing forth') are revelations of facets of Stephen's life, they 'show forth' something which remains in his consciousness. But they are not ecstatic, and the 'elevation' he receives from them can only be a long-term one and not anything immediate. But certainly Joyce registers the mystical moment, its significance as part of his hero's development, a seeing to the heart, the past's heritage for the present.

Finally, we must consider Joyce's use of the interior monologue *and* at the same time his detached appraisal of Stephen. These combined – and they are the stylistic heart of *A Portrait* – provide the balance that a fine work of art requires. Here is Joyce describing Stephen's holiday activity. This is straight objective narrative, though not without that tincture of irony which characterizes so much of Joyce's writing:

Then would begin Stephen's run round the park. Mike Flynn would stand at the gate near the railway station, watch in hand, while Stephen ran round the track in the style Mike Flynn favoured, his head high lifted, his knees well lifted and his hands held straight down by his sides. (*Chapter 2*, p.56)

This is conventional distanced description, a far cry from the main method of the novel which reveals Stephen from the inside. This is most effectively done in a seemingly disconnected way, as when Stephen's mind runs on before he is taken to the infirmary. The 'stream of consciousness' has little rocks which arrest its flow, but here is Joyce's method, the method of *Ulysses* in miniature:

The face and the voice went away. Sorry because he was afraid. Afraid that it was some disease. Canker was a disease of plants and cancer one of animals: or another different. That was a long time ago then out on the playgrounds in the evening light, creeping from point to point on the fringe of his line, a heavy bird flying low through the grey light. Leicester Abbey lit up. Wolsey died there. The abbots buried him themselves. (*Chapter 1*, p.20)

There is recall from the past, Wells shouldering Stephen into the ditch, and the rote-learning from Dr Cornwell's book, all jumbled in the mind of the sick child. The style is finely evocative, for all the things referred to have been planted in our minds earlier. The result is to involve us intimately with the feverish child, to show us his thought processes and emotional 'hang-ups' in action. It is the principal method of *A Portrait*, though the degree of consciousness or unconsciousness varies; Joyce was to perfect the device later by dispensing with punctuation, thus ensuring that the stream flowed freely, unimpeded by the dams of commas and full-stops.

In any section on style there will be omissions, and in a text as rich and as crowded with reference and innuendo as *A Portrait* one can only indicate the main techniques employed by Joyce. The *Textual notes* should be used as a supplement to this section, for they indicate the nature of the figurative language and its incidence, the employment of symbol, epiphany, irony, dialogue and interior monologue, as well as some of the original aspects of Joyce's mode of expression in this novel.

General questions and sample answer in note form

1 Write an account of Joyce's use of the *senses* in the first two chapters of *A Portrait*.

2 Find *three* examples of Joyce's use of the *epiphany* (apart from those mentioned in the section on *Style*), and write a critical appreciation of each.

3 What elements of *A Portrait* do you regard as 'poetic'? Quote in support of your views, and give reasons for your evaluation.

4 Write an essay on Joyce's use of irony or satire in this novel.

5 What aspects of Joyce's use of imagery interest you most in *A Portrait*, and why?

6 In what ways do you find Stephen an unsympathetic character? Give reasons for your answer.

7 Write a character sketch of either Mr Dedalus or Cranly. In what ways does either of them exert an influence upon Stephen?

8 Examine, by detailed reference to the text, Joyce's use of the 'interior monologue' in *A Portrait*.

9 Summarize in some detail Stephen's aesthetic and artistic theories in Chapter Five.

10 Summarize the main arguments of the 'hell-fire' sermons during the retreat, and indicate the effect they have on Stephen.

11 'Superbly the creator of atmosphere.' Would you agree with this estimate of Joyce's achievement in this novel?

12 What aspects of *A Portrait* do you find humorous, and why?

13 'Thoroughly unnatural and abnormal.' Would you agree with this assessment of Stephen's reactions in *A Portrait*?

14 Examine in some detail Joyce's use of the 'flashback' technique in *A Portrait*.

15 Write an essay on the structure of *A Portrait* with particular reference to the content of each of the five chapters.

16 In what way is dialogue important in *A Portrait*?

17 How far is a knowledge of any background information important to our appreciation of *A Portrait*?

18 How far is Joyce successful in conveying to us the quality of life in Dublin at the time?

19 'A controlled but bitter attack on Catholicism.' How far would you agree with this judgment of *A Portrait*?

20 Write an essay on Joyce's ability to portray *either* the sordid *or* the mystical in *A Portrait*.

21 In what ways is *A Portrait* unlike any other novel you have read?

22 Do you regard *A Portrait* as fundamentally optimistic or pessimistic? Give reasons for your answer.

23 Write an essay on Joyce's use of poetry and song in *A Portrait*.

24 'Overlaid with too much learning, too little feeling being allowed to get through to the reader.' Would you agree with this estimate of *A Portrait*?

25 'It is all words, inward and outward talk: not much happens.' Do you agree?

Suggested notes for essay answer to question 1

(a) *Introduction* – the senses – sight (or part-sight), hearing, touch, smell, etc. central to Joyce's conception, particularly important because of Stephen's sensitive nature – he responds to atmosphere throughout his life whether sordid or ecstatic; some epiphanies are sense perceptions or associations.

(b) Early childhood – smell (wetting the bed) plus touch – nice smell of mother; eyes weak at school; hands bluish with cold; contrast of lying before the fire and cold slimy water. Air in corridor, lavatory 'gas – like a little song' – pick out other instances.

(c) Smell in chapel – cold white sheets – home – noises of

welcome – warmth of forehead – fear of rats – sickness – weakness – breaking of spectacles; listening to cricketers; coolness of Eileen's hands – sense of other people's hands – sense of sin associated with touch and wine – caning and sensitivity re his own hands – end of chapter smells and sounds.

(d) Include and evaluate details in Chapter 2 in the manner given above.

(e) *Conclusion* – Stephen's senses always alert to reflex and other experiences – weak sight, stronger outward vision – sordid sights, sounds, smells part of his daily life at times – all contribute to the shaping of the artist.

Further reading

James Joyce, Richard Ellman (Oxford University Press). The definitive biography.

The Introduction by J. S. Atherton in *Portrait of the Artist as a Young Man* (Heinemann, Modern Novel series). The definitive edition of the book.

Joyce, John Gross (Fontana, Modern Masters series). A short study.

Essay by Edmund Wilson in *Axel's Castle* (Collins, Fontana Library).

Essay by J. I. M. Stewart in *Eight Modern Writers* (Oxford, History of English Literature series).

'Dubliners' and 'A Portrait of the Artist as a Young Man', – *A Selection of Critical Essays*, Ed. Morris Beja (Macmillan, Casebook series). Good background material.

Brodie's Notes

D. H. Lawrence	**The Rainbow**
D. H. Lawrence	**Sons and Lovers**
D. H. Lawrence	**Women in Love**
Harper Lee	**To Kill a Mockingbird**
Laurie Lee	**Cider with Rosie**
Christopher Marlowe	**Dr Faustus**
Arthur Miller	**The Crucible**
Arthur Miller	**Death of a Salesman**
John Milton	**Paradise Lost**
Robert C. O'Brien	**Z for Zachariah**
Sean O'Casey	**Juno and the Paycock**
George Orwell	**Animal Farm**
George Orwell	**1984**
J. B. Priestley	**An Inspector Calls**
J. D. Salinger	**The Catcher in the Rye**
William Shakespeare	**Antony and Cleopatra**
William Shakespeare	**As You Like It**
William Shakespeare	**Hamlet**
William Shakespeare	**Henry IV Part I**
William Shakespeare	**Julius Caesar**
William Shakespeare	**King Lear**
William Shakespeare	**Macbeth**
William Shakespeare	**Measure for Measure**
William Shakespeare	**The Merchant of Venice**
William Shakespeare	**A Midsummer Night's Dream**
William Shakespeare	**Much Ado about Nothing**
William Shakespeare	**Othello**
William Shakespeare	**Richard II**
William Shakespeare	**Romeo and Juliet**
William Shakespeare	**The Tempest**
William Shakespeare	**Twelfth Night**
George Bernard Shaw	**Pygmalion**
Alan Sillitoe	**Selected Fiction**
John Steinbeck	**Of Mice and Men** and **The Pearl**
Jonathan Swift	**Gulliver's Travels**
Dylan Thomas	**Under Milk Wood**
Alice Walker	**The Color Purple**
W. B. Yeats	**Selected Poetry**

ENGLISH COURSEWORK BOOKS

Terri Apter	**Women and Society**
Kevin Dowling	**Drama and Poetry**
Philip Gooden	**Conflict**
Philip Gooden	**Science Fiction**
Margaret K. Gray	**Modern Drama**
Graham Handley	**Modern Poetry**
Graham Handley	**Prose**
Graham Handley	**Childhood and Adolescence**
R. J. Sims	**The Short Story**